QUIET

ONE YEAR DAILY DEVOTIONAL FOR STUDENTS

TIME

QUIET TIME
ONE YEAR DAILY DEVOTIONAL FOR STUDENTS

Word of Life Local Church Ministries
A division of Word of Life Fellowship, Inc.
Joe Jordan – Executive Director
Don Lough – Director
Jack Wyrtzen & Harry Bollback – Founders
Ric Garland – VP of Local Church Ministries

USA
P.O. Box 600
Schroon Lake, NY 12870
talk@wol.org
1-888-932-5827

Canada
RR#8/Owen Sound
ON, Canada N4K 5W4
LCM@wol.ca
1-800-461-3503

Web Address: www.wol.org

Publisher's Acknowledgements
Writers and Contributors:

Glenn Amos	Romans
Bobby Barton	2 Corinthians, 2 Samuel, Hosea, Isaiah
Cory Fehr	Luke (Chapters 1-11)
Dave Huizing	1 Samuel, Psalms
Paul O' Bradovic	1 Peter, James, Philippians
Joe and Gloria Phillips	Proverbs
Matt Walls	Luke (Chapters 12-24)
Lindsey Young	Ezekiel

Editor: Dale Flynn
Curriculum Manager: Don Reichard
Cover and page design: Boire Design, Inc.

ISBN - 978-1-935475-14-9
Printed in the United States of America

helpful hints for a daily QUIET TIME

The purpose of this Quiet Time is to meet the needs of spiritual growth in the life of the Christian in such a way that they learn the art of conducting their own personal investigation into the Bible.

Consider the following helpful hints:

1 Give priority in choosing your quiet time. This will vary with each individual in accordance with his own circumstances. The time you choose must:

- have top priority over everything else
- be the quietest time possible.
- be a convenient time of the day or night.
- be consistently observed each day.

2 Give attention to the procedure suggested for you to follow. Include the following items.

- Read God's Word.
- Mark your Bible as you read. Here are some suggestions that might be helpful:
  a. After you read the passage put an exclamation mark next to the verses you completely understand.
  b. Put a question mark next to verses you do not understand.
  c. Put an arrow pointing upward next to encouraging verses.
  d. Put an arrow pointing downward next to verses which weigh us down in our spiritual race.
  e. Put a star next to verses containing important truths or major points.
- Meditate on what you have read (In one sentence, write the main thought). Here are some suggestions as guidelines for meditating on God's Word:
  a. Look at the selected passage from God's point of view.

b. Though we encourage quiet time in the morning, some people arrange to have their quiet time at the end of their day. God emphasizes that we need to go to sleep meditating on His Word. "My soul shall be satisfied and my mouth shall praise thee with joyful lips: when I remember thee upon my bed, and meditating on thee in the night watches" (Psalm 63:5,6).

c. Deuteronomy 6:7 lists routine things you do each day during which you should concentrate on the portion of Scripture for that day:
— when you sit in your house (meals and relaxation)
— when you walk in the way (to and from school or work)
— when you lie down (before going to sleep at night)
— when you rise up (getting ready for the day)

■ Apply some truth to your life. (Use first person pronouns I, me, my, mine). If you have difficulty in finding an application for your life, think of yourself as a Bible SPECTator and ask yourself the following questions.

S – is there any sin for me to forsake?

P – is there any promise for me to claim?

E – is there any example for me to follow?

C – is there any command for me to obey?

T – is there anything to be thankful for today?

■ Pray for specific things (Use the prayer sheets found in the My Prayer Journal section).

3 Be sure to fill out your quiet time sheets. This will really help you remember the things the Lord brings to your mind.

4 Purpose to share with someone else each day something you gained from your quiet time. This can be a real blessing for them as well as for you.

Step by step through
QuietTime

The Quiet Time for Students will help you have a special time each day with the Lord. The daily passages are organized so that you cover every book of the Bible in six years. All Word of Life quiet times use the same daily passage for all ages, so families, small groups, or even entire churches can encourage each other from the Word of God.

The following instructions walk you through the steps for using the Quiet Time.

> First read the weekly overview to learn what the focus is for the coming week.

Week 4

Are you ready for an extreme makeover? We all have our ideas about how we would like to look, but God has His own plans for us. At the end of this week's Quiet Time, the new you will be revealed. Who will you look like after God does an extreme makeover on you?

prayer focus for this week

> Use this area to write prayer requests and reminders for the week.

the Question
the Answer

What is the writer saying?

How can I apply this to my life?

Sunday   2 Corinthians 1:1-11

Q

A

> Next, listen to the Lord as you read the daily passage.

Diggi ... you doing this to me, God?" If you have not aske̶d ... ̶bly will. Today we start the book of 2 Corinthians. P̶a ... 19:23-20:3), and he knew that God always had a pu̶ ... at we can comfort others (v. 4). We have trouble so ... ̶e who is having a hard time (v. 6). There's a saying, ... God brings you through the trouble you are having, you will soon discover others who are also having trouble, and you can be an encouragement to them.

> Now share your thoughts as you answer the two questions.

helpful hints for a
daily QUIET TIME

monday 2 Corinthians 1:12-24

Digging Deeper • Have you ever been falsely accused? Paul had written the book of 1 Corinthians to the church in Corinth one year before, and now he [...] letter. He talks about his conscience being honest before the [...] asked the church for sin that was allowed to continue; now he [...] (v. 14). Paul had to defend his truthfulness in verses 15-20 [...] and words had been reliable, just as all the promises of God [...]. Paul was honest before God the Father, Son, and Holy [...] himself as a fellow helper to the Corinthian believers. [...] thought about God? **What do you think he thought about himself? What do you think he thought about other people? How would you answer these questions about yourself?**

> *Take time to read the Digging Deeper commentary for additional insights on the text.*

tuesday 2 Corinthians 2:1-13

Digging Deeper • False teachers had lied about Paul to the church in Corinth. Now Paul tells the church why he had not come back to see them. His love for them caused him to stay away [...] correct the sin in the church. This love motivat[...] tells them to forgive the man who had sinned [...] fellowship. Once we ask God and fellow Christi[...] that person. Paul is also showing his need for Christian fellowship (2-13)—he needed encouragement from Titus, and he went looking for him. **Have you forgiven someone who has sinned against you? How many reasons for forgiveness can you find in today's verses?**

> *Consider these questions as you begin your prayer time.*

> *Use the weekly and daily prayer pages in the front of the Quiet Time to organize your prayer time as God leads you.*

my personal
prayer journal

Sunday

family

christian friends

unsaved friends

missionaries

monday

family

christian friends

unsaved friends

missionaries

tuesday

family

christian friends

unsaved friends

missionaries

Wednesday

family

christian friends

unsaved friends

missionaries

thursday

family

christian friends

unsaved friends

missionaries

friday

family

christian friends

unsaved friends

missionaries

saturday

family

christian friends

unsaved friends

missionaries

praise List

praise List

praise List

praise List

praise List

Some people just can't get enough! That is why we have several dimensions in the Word of Life Quiet Time. Along with the daily reading, content and application questions for each day, two reading programs are given to help you understand the Bible better. Choose one or both.

Reading Through the New Testament Four Times In One Year

Turn the page and discover a schedule that takes you through the New Testament four times in one year. This is a great method to help you see the correlation of the Gospels and other New Testament books.

Reading Through the Whole Bible In One Year

Turn another page and find a program of several pages that will guide you through a chronological reading of the entire Bible. Follow this schedule and you will move from Genesis through Revelation in one year.

The Choice is Up to You

Whether you have a short quiet time, a quiet time with more scripture reading or one with a mini-Bible study each day, we trust your time with God will draw you closer to Him in every area of your life.

Read through the new testament four times in one year

Weeks 1-13

- ☐ Matthew 1-3
- ☐ Matthew 4-6
- ☐ Matthew 7-9
- ☐ Matt. 10-12
- ☐ Matt. 13-15
- ☐ Matt. 16-18
- ☐ Matt. 19-21
- ☐ Matt. 22-24
- ☐ Matt. 25-26
- ☐ Matt. 27-28
- ☐ Mark 1-3
- ☐ Mark 4-5
- ☐ Mark 6-8
- ☐ Mark 9-11
- ☐ Mark 12-14
- ☐ Mark 15-16
- ☐ Luke 1-2
- ☐ Luke 3-5
- ☐ Luke 6-7
- ☐ Luke 8-9
- ☐ Luke 10-11
- ☐ Luke 12-14
- ☐ Luke 15-17
- ☐ Luke 18-20
- ☐ Luke 21-22
- ☐ Luke 23-24
- ☐ John 1-3
- ☐ John 4-5
- ☐ John 6-7
- ☐ John 8-10
- ☐ John 11-12
- ☐ John 13-15
- ☐ John 16-18
- ☐ John 19-21
- ☐ Acts 1-3
- ☐ Acts 4-6
- ☐ Acts 7-8
- ☐ Acts 9-11
- ☐ Acts 12-15
- ☐ Acts 16-18
- ☐ Acts 19-21
- ☐ Acts 22-24
- ☐ Acts 25-26
- ☐ Acts 27-28
- ☐ Romans 1-3

- ☐ Romans 4-6
- ☐ Romans 7-9
- ☐ Romans 10-12
- ☐ Romans 13-16
- ☐ 1 Cor. 1-4
- ☐ 1 Cor. 5-9
- ☐ 1 Cor. 10-12
- ☐ 1 Cor. 13-16
- ☐ 2 Cor. 1-4
- ☐ 2 Cor. 5-8
- ☐ 2 Cor. 9-13
- ☐ Galatians 1-3
- ☐ Galatians 4-6
- ☐ Ephesians 1-3
- ☐ Ephesians 4-6
- ☐ Philippians 1-4
- ☐ Colossians 1-4
- ☐ 1 Thes. 1-3
- ☐ 1 Thes. 4-5
- ☐ 2 Thes. 1-3
- ☐ 1 Timothy 1-3
- ☐ 1 Timothy 4-6
- ☐ 2 Timothy 1-4
- ☐ Titus 1-3
- ☐ Philemon
- ☐ Hebrews 1
- ☐ Hebrews 2-4
- ☐ Hebrews 5-7
- ☐ Hebrews 8-10
- ☐ Hebrews 11-13
- ☐ James 1-3
- ☐ James 4-5
- ☐ 1 Peter 1-3
- ☐ 1 Peter 4-5
- ☐ 2 Peter 1-3
- ☐ 1 John 1-3
- ☐ 1 John 4-5
- ☐ 2 Jn, 3 Jn, Jude
- ☐ Revelation 1-3
- ☐ Revelation 4-6
- ☐ Revelation 7-9
- ☐ Rev. 10-12
- ☐ Rev. 13-15
- ☐ Rev. 16-18
- ☐ Rev. 19-22

Weeks 14-26

- ☐ Matthew 1-3
- ☐ Matthew 4-6
- ☐ Matthew 7-9
- ☐ Matt. 10-12
- ☐ Matt. 13-15
- ☐ Matt. 16-18
- ☐ Matt. 19-21
- ☐ Matt. 22-24
- ☐ Matt. 25-26
- ☐ Matt. 27-28
- ☐ Mark 1-3
- ☐ Mark 4-5
- ☐ Mark 6-8
- ☐ Mark 9-11
- ☐ Mark 12-14
- ☐ Mark 15-16
- ☐ Luke 1-2
- ☐ Luke 3-5
- ☐ Luke 6-7
- ☐ Luke 8-9
- ☐ Luke 10-11
- ☐ Luke 12-14
- ☐ Luke 15-17
- ☐ Luke 18-20
- ☐ Luke 21-22
- ☐ Luke 23-24
- ☐ John 1-3
- ☐ John 4-5
- ☐ John 6-7
- ☐ John 8-10
- ☐ John 11-12
- ☐ John 13-15
- ☐ John 16-18
- ☐ John 19-21
- ☐ Acts 1-3
- ☐ Acts 4-6
- ☐ Acts 7-8
- ☐ Acts 9-11
- ☐ Acts 12-15
- ☐ Acts 16-18
- ☐ Acts 19-21
- ☐ Acts 22-24
- ☐ Acts 25-26
- ☐ Acts 27-28
- ☐ Romans 1-3

- ☐ Romans 4-6
- ☐ Romans 7-9
- ☐ Romans 10-12
- ☐ Romans 13-16
- ☐ 1 Cor. 1-4
- ☐ 1 Cor. 5-9
- ☐ 1 Cor. 10-12
- ☐ 1 Cor. 13-16
- ☐ 2 Cor. 1-4
- ☐ 2 Cor. 5-8
- ☐ 2 Cor. 9-13
- ☐ Galatians 1-3
- ☐ Galatians 4-6
- ☐ Ephesians 1-3
- ☐ Ephesians 4-6
- ☐ Philippians 1-4
- ☐ Colossians 1-4
- ☐ 1 Thes. 1-3
- ☐ 1 Thes. 4-5
- ☐ 2 Thes. 1-3
- ☐ 1 Timothy 1-3
- ☐ 1 Timothy 4-6
- ☐ 2 Timothy 1-4
- ☐ Titus 1-3
- ☐ Philemon
- ☐ Hebrews 1
- ☐ Hebrews 2-4
- ☐ Hebrews 5-7
- ☐ Hebrews 8-10
- ☐ Hebrews 11-13
- ☐ James 1-3
- ☐ James 4-5
- ☐ 1 Peter 1-3
- ☐ 1 Peter 4-5
- ☐ 2 Peter 1-3
- ☐ 1 John 1-3
- ☐ 1 John 4-5
- ☐ 2 Jn, 3 Jn, Jude
- ☐ Revelation 1-3
- ☐ Revelation 4-6
- ☐ Revelation 7-9
- ☐ Rev. 10-12
- ☐ Rev. 13-15
- ☐ Rev. 16-18
- ☐ Rev. 19-22

Read through the new testament four times in one year

Weeks 27-39

- [ ] Matthew 1-3
- [ ] Matthew 4-6
- [ ] Matthew 7-9
- [ ] Matt. 10-12
- [ ] Matt. 13-15
- [ ] Matt. 16-18
- [ ] Matt. 19-21
- [ ] Matt. 22-24
- [ ] Matt. 25-26
- [ ] Matt. 27-28
- [ ] Mark 1-3
- [ ] Mark 4-5
- [ ] Mark 6-8
- [ ] Mark 9-11
- [ ] Mark 12-14
- [ ] Mark 15-16
- [ ] Luke 1-2
- [ ] Luke 3-5
- [ ] Luke 6-7
- [ ] Luke 8-9
- [ ] Luke 10-11
- [ ] Luke 12-14
- [ ] Luke 15-17
- [ ] Luke 18-20
- [ ] Luke 21-22
- [ ] Luke 23-24
- [ ] John 1-3
- [ ] John 4-5
- [ ] John 6-7
- [ ] John 8-10
- [ ] John 11-12
- [ ] John 13-15
- [ ] John 16-18
- [ ] John 19-21
- [ ] Acts 1-3
- [ ] Acts 4-6
- [ ] Acts 7-8
- [ ] Acts 9-11
- [ ] Acts 12-15
- [ ] Acts 16-18
- [ ] Acts 19-21
- [ ] Acts 22-24
- [ ] Acts 25-26
- [ ] Acts 27-28
- [ ] Romans 1-3

- [ ] Romans 4-6
- [ ] Romans 7-9
- [ ] Romans 10-12
- [ ] Romans 13-16
- [ ] 1 Cor. 1-4
- [ ] 1 Cor. 5-9
- [ ] 1 Cor. 10-12
- [ ] 1 Cor. 13-16
- [ ] 2 Cor. 1-4
- [ ] 2 Cor. 5-8
- [ ] 2 Cor. 9-13
- [ ] Galatians 1-3
- [ ] Galatians 4-6
- [ ] Ephesians 1-3
- [ ] Ephesians 4-6
- [ ] Phil. 1-4
- [ ] Colossians 1-4
- [ ] 1 Thes. 1-3
- [ ] 1 Thes. 4-5
- [ ] 2 Thes. 1-3
- [ ] 1 Timothy 1-3
- [ ] 1 Timothy 4-6
- [ ] 2 Timothy 1-4
- [ ] Titus 1-3
- [ ] Philemon
- [ ] Hebrews 1
- [ ] Hebrews 2-4
- [ ] Hebrews 5-7
- [ ] Hebrews 8-10
- [ ] Hebrews 11-13
- [ ] James 1-3
- [ ] James 4-5
- [ ] 1 Peter 1-3
- [ ] 1 Peter 4-5
- [ ] 2 Peter 1-3
- [ ] 1 John 1-3
- [ ] 1 John 4-5
- [ ] 2 Jn, 3 Jn, Jude
- [ ] Revelation 1-3
- [ ] Revelation 4-6
- [ ] Revelation 7-9
- [ ] Rev. 10-12
- [ ] Rev. 13-15
- [ ] Rev. 16-18
- [ ] Rev. 19-22

Weeks 40-52

- [ ] Matthew 1-3
- [ ] Matthew 4-6
- [ ] Matthew 7-9
- [ ] Matt. 10-12
- [ ] Matt. 13-15
- [ ] Matt. 16-18
- [ ] Matt. 19-21
- [ ] Matt. 22-24
- [ ] Matt. 25-26
- [ ] Matt. 27-28
- [ ] Mark 1-3
- [ ] Mark 4-5
- [ ] Mark 6-8
- [ ] Mark 9-11
- [ ] Mark 12-14
- [ ] Mark 15-16
- [ ] Luke 1-2
- [ ] Luke 3-5
- [ ] Luke 6-7
- [ ] Luke 8-9
- [ ] Luke 10-11
- [ ] Luke 12-14
- [ ] Luke 15-17
- [ ] Luke 18-20
- [ ] Luke 21-22
- [ ] Luke 23-24
- [ ] John 1-3
- [ ] John 4-5
- [ ] John 6-7
- [ ] John 8-10
- [ ] John 11-12
- [ ] John 13-15
- [ ] John 16-18
- [ ] John 19-21
- [ ] Acts 1-3
- [ ] Acts 4-6
- [ ] Acts 7-8
- [ ] Acts 9-11
- [ ] Acts 12-15
- [ ] Acts 16-18
- [ ] Acts 19-21
- [ ] Acts 22-24
- [ ] Acts 25-26
- [ ] Acts 27-28
- [ ] Romans 1-3

- [ ] Romans 4-6
- [ ] Romans 7-9
- [ ] Romans 10-12
- [ ] Romans 13-16
- [ ] 1 Cor. 1-4
- [ ] 1 Cor. 5-9
- [ ] 1 Cor. 10-12
- [ ] 1 Cor. 13-16
- [ ] 2 Cor. 1-4
- [ ] 2 Cor. 5-8
- [ ] 2 Cor. 9-13
- [ ] Galatians 1-3
- [ ] Galatians 4-6
- [ ] Ephesians 1-3
- [ ] Ephesians 4-6
- [ ] Phil. 1-4
- [ ] Colossians 1-4
- [ ] 1 Thes. 1-3
- [ ] 1 Thes. 4-5
- [ ] 2 Thes. 1-3
- [ ] 1 Timothy 1-3
- [ ] 1 Timothy 4-6
- [ ] 2 Timothy 1-4
- [ ] Titus 1-3
- [ ] Philemon
- [ ] Hebrews 1
- [ ] Hebrews 2-4
- [ ] Hebrews 5-7
- [ ] Hebrews 8-10
- [ ] Hebrews 11-13
- [ ] James 1-3
- [ ] James 4-5
- [ ] 1 Peter 1-3
- [ ] 1 Peter 4-5
- [ ] 2 Peter 1-3
- [ ] 1 John 1-3
- [ ] 1 John 4-5
- [ ] 2 Jn, 3 Jn, Jude
- [ ] Revelation 1-3
- [ ] Revelation 4-6
- [ ] Revelation 7-9
- [ ] Rev. 10-12
- [ ] Rev. 13-15
- [ ] Rev. 16-18
- [ ] Rev. 19-22

Bible reading schedule

Read through the Bible in one year! As you complete each daily reading, simply place a check in the appropriate box.

- ☐ 1 Genesis 1-3
- ☐ 2 Genesis 4:1-6:8
- ☐ 3 Genesis 6:9-9:29
- ☐ 4 Genesis 10-11
- ☐ 5 Genesis 12-14
- ☐ 6 Genesis 15-17
- ☐ 7 Genesis 18-19
- ☐ 8 Genesis 20-22
- ☐ 9 Genesis 23-24
- ☐ 10 Genesis 25-26
- ☐ 11 Genesis 27-28
- ☐ 12 Genesis 29-30
- ☐ 13 Genesis 31-32
- ☐ 14 Genesis 33-35
- ☐ 15 Genesis 36-37
- ☐ 16 Genesis 38-40
- ☐ 17 Genesis 41-42
- ☐ 18 Genesis 43-45
- ☐ 19 Genesis 46-47
- ☐ 20 Genesis 48-50
- ☐ 21 Job 1-3
- ☐ 22 Job 4-7
- ☐ 23 Job 8-11
- ☐ 24 Job 12-15
- ☐ 25 Job 16-19
- ☐ 26 Job 20-22
- ☐ 27 Job 23-28
- ☐ 28 Job 29-31
- ☐ 29 Job 32-34
- ☐ 30 Job 35-37
- ☐ 31 Job 38-42
- ☐ 32 Exodus 1-4
- ☐ 33 Exodus 5-8
- ☐ 34 Exodus 9-11
- ☐ 35 Exodus 12-13
- ☐ 36 Exodus 14-15
- ☐ 37 Exodus 16-18
- ☐ 38 Exodus 19-21
- ☐ 39 Exodus 22-24
- ☐ 40 Exodus 25-27
- ☐ 41 Exodus 28-29
- ☐ 42 Exodus 30-31
- ☐ 43 Exodus 32-34
- ☐ 44 Exodus 35-36
- ☐ 45 Exodus 37-38
- ☐ 46 Exodus 39-40
- ☐ 47 Leviticus 1:1-5:13
- ☐ 48 Leviticus 5:14-7:38
- ☐ 49 Leviticus 8-10
- ☐ 50 Leviticus 11-12
- ☐ 51 Leviticus 13-14
- ☐ 52 Leviticus 15-17
- ☐ 53 Leviticus 18-20
- ☐ 54 Leviticus 21-23
- ☐ 55 Leviticus 24-25
- ☐ 56 Leviticus 26-27
- ☐ 57 Numbers 1-2
- ☐ 58 Numbers 3-4
- ☐ 59 Numbers 5-6
- ☐ 60 Numbers 7
- ☐ 61 Numbers 8-10
- ☐ 62 Numbers 11-13
- ☐ 63 Numbers 14-15
- ☐ 64 Numbers 16-18
- ☐ 65 Numbers 19-21
- ☐ 66 Numbers 22-24
- ☐ 67 Numbers 25-26
- ☐ 68 Numbers 27-29
- ☐ 69 Numbers 30-31
- ☐ 70 Numbers 32-33
- ☐ 71 Numbers 34-36
- ☐ 72 Deuteronomy 1-2
- ☐ 73 Deuteronomy 3-4
- ☐ 74 Deuteronomy 5-7
- ☐ 75 Deuteronomy 8-10
- ☐ 76 Deuteronomy 11-13
- ☐ 77 Deuteronomy 14-17
- ☐ 78 Deuteronomy 18-21
- ☐ 79 Deuteronomy 22-25
- ☐ 80 Deuteronomy 26-28
- ☐ 81 Deuteronomy 29:1-31:29
- ☐ 82 Deuteronomy 31:30-34:12
- ☐ 83 Joshua 1-4
- ☐ 84 Joshua 5-8
- ☐ 85 Joshua 9-11
- ☐ 86 Joshua 12-14
- ☐ 87 Joshua 15-17
- ☐ 88 Joshua 18-19
- ☐ 89 Joshua 20-22
- ☐ 90 Joshua 23 - Judges 1
- ☐ 91 Judges 2-5
- ☐ 92 Judges 6-8
- ☐ 93 Judges 9
- ☐ 94 Judges 10-12
- ☐ 95 Judges 13-16
- ☐ 96 Judges 17-19
- ☐ 97 Judges 20-21
- ☐ 98 Ruth
- ☐ 99 1 Samuel 1-3
- ☐ 100 1 Samuel 4-7
- ☐ 101 1 Samuel 8-10
- ☐ 102 1 Samuel 11-13
- ☐ 103 1 Samuel 14-15
- ☐ 104 1 Samuel 16-17

Bible reading schedule

- [ ] 105 1 Samuel 18-19; Psalm 59
- [ ] 106 1 Samuel 20-21; Psalm 56; 34
- [ ] 107 1 Samuel 22-23; 1 Chronicles 12:8-18; Psalm 52; 54; 63; 142
- [ ] 108 1 Samuel 24; Psalm 57; 1 Samuel 25
- [ ] 109 1 Samuel 26-29; 1 Chronicles 12:1-7, 19-22
- [ ] 110 1 Samuel 30-31; 1 Chronicles 10; 2 Samuel 1
- [ ] 111 2 Samuel 2-4
- [ ] 112 2 Samuel 5:1-6:11; 1 Chronicles 11:1-9; 2:23-40; 13:1-14:17
- [ ] 113 2 Samuel 22; Psalm 18
- [ ] 114 1 Chronicles 15-16; 2 Samuel 6:12-23; Psalm 96
- [ ] 115 Psalm 105; 2 Samuel 7; 1 Chronicles 17
- [ ] 116 2 Samuel 8-10; 1 Chronicles 18-19; Psalm 60
- [ ] 117 2 Samuel 11-12; 1 Chronicles 20:1-3; Psalm 51
- [ ] 118 2 Samuel 13-14
- [ ] 119 2 Samuel 15-17
- [ ] 120 Psalm 3; 2 Samuel 18-19
- [ ] 121 2 Samuel 20-21; 23:8-23; 1 Chronicles 20:4-8; 11:10-25
- [ ] 122 2 Samuel 23:24-24:25;
- [ ] 123 1 Chronicles 11:26-47; 21:1-30, 1 Chronicles 22-24
- [ ] 124 Psalm 30; 1 Chronicles 25-26
- [ ] 125 1 Chronicles 27-29
- [ ] 126 Psalms 5-7; 10; 11; 13; 17
- [ ] 127 Psalms 23; 26; 28; 31; 35
- [ ] 128 Psalms 41; 43; 46; 55; 61; 62; 64
- [ ] 129 Psalms 69-71; 77
- [ ] 130 Psalms 83; 86; 88; 91; 95
- [ ] 131 Psalms 108-9; 120-21; 140; 143-44
- [ ] 132 Psalms 1; 14-15; 36-37; 39
- [ ] 133 Psalms 40; 49-50; 73
- [ ] 134 Psalms 76; 82; 84; 90; 92; 112; 115
- [ ] 135 Psalms 8-9; 16; 19; 21; 24; 29
- [ ] 136 Psalms 33; 65-68
- [ ] 137 Psalms 75; 93-94; 97-100
- [ ] 138 Psalms 103-4; 113-14; 117
- [ ] 139 Psalm 119:1-88
- [ ] 140 Psalm 119:89-176
- [ ] 141 Psalms 122; 124; 133-36
- [ ] 142 Psalms 138-39; 145; 148; 150
- [ ] 143 Psalms 4; 12; 20; 25; 32; 38
- [ ] 144 Psalms 42; 53; 58; 81; 101; 111; 130-31;141;146
- [ ] 145 Psalms 2; 22; 27
- [ ] 146 Psalms 45; 47-48; 87; 110
- [ ] 147 1 Kings 1:1-2:12; 2 Samuel 23:1-7
- [ ] 148 1 Kings 2:13-3:28; 2 Chronicles 1:1-13
- [ ] 149 1 Kings 5-6; 2 Chronicles 2-3
- [ ] 150 1 Kings 7; 2 Chronicles 4
- [ ] 151 1 Kings 8; 2 Chronicles 5:1-7:10
- [ ] 152 1 Kings 9:1-10:13; 2 Chronicles 7:11-9:12
- [ ] 153 1 Kings 4; 10:14-29; 2 Chronicles 1:14-17; 9:13-28; Psalm 72
- [ ] 154 Proverbs 1-3
- [ ] 155 Proverbs 4-6
- [ ] 156 Proverbs 7-9
- [ ] 157 Proverbs 10-12
- [ ] 158 Proverbs 13-15
- [ ] 159 Proverbs 16-18
- [ ] 160 Proverbs 19-21
- [ ] 161 Proverbs 22-24
- [ ] 162 Proverbs 25-27
- [ ] 163 Proverbs 28-29
- [ ] 164 Proverbs 30-31; Psalm 127
- [ ] 165 Song of Solomon
- [ ] 166 1 Kings 11:1-40; Ecclesiastes 1-2
- [ ] 167 Ecclesiastes 3-7
- [ ] 168 Ecclesiastes 8-12; 1 Kings 11:41-43; 2 Chronicles 9:29-31
- [ ] 169 1 Kings 12; 2 Chronicles 10:1-11:17
- [ ] 170 1 Kings 13-14; 2 Chronicles 11:18-12:16
- [ ] 171 1 Kings 15:1-24; 2 Chronicles 13-16
- [ ] 172 1 Kings 15:25-16:34; 2 Chronicles 17; 1 Kings 17
- [ ] 173 1 Kings 18-19
- [ ] 174 1 Kings 20-21
- [ ] 175 1 Kings 22:1-40; 2 Chronicles 18
- [ ] 176 1 Kings 22:41-53; 2 Kings 1; 2 Chronicles 19:1-21:3
- [ ] 177 2 Kings 2-4
- [ ] 178 2 Kings 5-7
- [ ] 179 2 Kings 8-9; 2 Chronicles 21:4-22:9
- [ ] 180 2 Kings 10-11; 2 Chronicles 22:10-23:21
- [ ] 181 Joel
- [ ] 182 2 Kings 12-13; 2 Chronicles 24
- [ ] 183 2 Kings 14; 2 Chronicles 25; Jonah
- [ ] 184 Hosea 1-7
- [ ] 185 Hosea 8-14
- [ ] 186 2 Kings 15:1-7; 2 Chronicles 26; Amos 1-4
- [ ] 187 Amos 5-9; 2 Kings 15:8-18
- [ ] 188 Isaiah 1-4
- [ ] 189 2 Kings 15:19-38; 2 Chronicles 27; Isaiah 5-6
- [ ] 190 Micah
- [ ] 191 2 Kings 16; 2 Chronicles 28; Isaiah 7-8
- [ ] 192 Isaiah 9-12
- [ ] 193 Isaiah 13-16
- [ ] 194 Isaiah 17-22
- [ ] 195 Isaiah 23-27
- [ ] 196 Isaiah 28-30
- [ ] 197 Isaiah 31-35
- [ ] 198 2 Kings 18:1-8; 2 Chronicles 29-31
- [ ] 199 2 Kings 17; 18:9-37; 2 Chronicles 32:1-19; Isaiah 36

Bible reading schedule

- ☐ 200 2 Kings 19; 2 Chronicles 32:20-23; Isaiah 37
- ☐ 201 2 Kings 20; 2 Chronicles 32:24-33; Isaiah 38-39
- ☐ 202 2 Kings 21:1-18; 2 Chronicles 33:1-20; Isaiah 40
- ☐ 203 Isaiah 41-43
- ☐ 204 Isaiah 44-47
- ☐ 205 Isaiah 48-51
- ☐ 206 Isaiah 52-57
- ☐ 207 Isaiah 58-62
- ☐ 208 Isaiah 63-66
- ☐ 209 2 Kings 21:19-26; 2 Chronicles 33:21-34:7; Zephaniah
- ☐ 210 Jeremiah 1-3
- ☐ 211 Jeremiah 4-6
- ☐ 212 Jeremiah 7-9
- ☐ 213 Jeremiah 10-13
- ☐ 214 Jeremiah 14-16
- ☐ 215 Jeremiah 17-20
- ☐ 216 2 Kings 22:1-23:28; 2 Chronicles 34:8-35:19
- ☐ 217 Nahum; 2 Kings 23:29-37;
- ☐ 2 Chronicles 35:20-36:5; Jeremiah 22:10-17
- ☐ 218 Jeremiah 26; Habakkuk
- ☐ 219 Jeremiah 46-47; 2 Kings 24:1-4, 7; 2 Chronicles 36:6-7; Jeremiah 25, 35
- ☐ 220 Jeremiah 36, 45, 48
- ☐ 221 Jeremiah 49:1-33; Daniel 1-2
- ☐ 222 Jeremiah 22:18-30; 2 Kings 24:5-20; 2 Chronicles 36:8-12; Jeremiah 37:1-2; 52:1-3; 24; 29
- ☐ 223 Jeremiah 27-28, 23
- ☐ 224 Jeremiah 50-51
- ☐ 225 Jeremiah 49:34-39; 34:1-22; Ezekiel 1-3
- ☐ 226 Ezekiel 4-7
- ☐ 227 Ezekiel 8-11
- ☐ 228 Ezekiel 12-14
- ☐ 229 Ezekiel 15-17
- ☐ 230 Ezekiel 18-20
- ☐ 231 Ezekiel 21-23
- ☐ 232 2 Kings 25:1; 2 Chronicles 36:13-16; Jeremiah 39:1; 52:4; Ezekiel 24; Jeremiah 21:1-22:9; 32:1-44
- ☐ 233 Jeremiah 30-31, 33
- ☐ 234 Ezekiel 25; 29:1-16; 30; 31
- ☐ 235 Ezekiel 26-28
- ☐ 236 Jeremiah 37:3-39:10; 52:5-30; 2 Kings 25:2-21; 2 Chronicles 36:17-21
- ☐ 237 2 Kings 25:22; Jeremiah 39:11-40:6; Lamentations 1-3
- ☐ 238 Lamentations 4-5; Obadiah
- ☐ 239 Jeremiah 40:7-44:30; 2 Kings 25:23-26
- ☐ 240 Ezekiel 33:21-36:38
- ☐ 241 Ezekiel 37-39
- ☐ 242 Ezekiel 32:1-33:20; Daniel 3
- ☐ 243 Ezekiel 40-42
- ☐ 244 Ezekiel 43-45
- ☐ 245 Ezekiel 46-48
- ☐ 246 Ezekiel 29:17-21; Daniel 4; Jeremiah 52:31-34; 2 Kings 25:27-30; Psalm 44
- ☐ 247 Psalms 74; 79-80; 89
- ☐ 248 Psalms 85; 102; 106; 123; 137
- ☐ 249 Daniel 7-8; 5
- ☐ 250 Daniel 9; 6
- ☐ 251 2 Chronicles 36:22-23; Ezra 1:1-4:5
- ☐ 252 Daniel 10-12
- ☐ 253 Ezra 4:6-6:13; Haggai
- ☐ 254 Zechariah 1-6
- ☐ 255 Zechariah 7-8; Ezra 6:14-22; Psalm 78
- ☐ 256 Psalms 107; 116; 118
- ☐ 257 Psalms 125-26; 128-29; 132; 147; 149
- ☐ 258 Zechariah 9-14
- ☐ 259 Esther 1-4
- ☐ 260 Esther 5-10
- ☐ 261 Ezra 7-8
- ☐ 262 Ezra 9-10
- ☐ 263 Nehemiah 1-5
- ☐ 264 Nehemiah 6-7
- ☐ 265 Nehemiah 8-10
- ☐ 266 Nehemiah 11-13
- ☐ 267 Malachi
- ☐ 268 1 Chronicles 1-2
- ☐ 269 1 Chronicles 3-5
- ☐ 270 1 Chronicles 6
- ☐ 271 1 Chronicles 7:1-8:27
- ☐ 272 1 Chronicles 8:28-9:44
- ☐ 273 John 1:1-18; Mark 1:1; Luke 1:1-4; 3:23-38; Matthew 1:1-17
- ☐ 274 Luke 1:5-80
- ☐ 275 Matthew 1:18-2:23; Luke 2
- ☐ 276 Matthew 3:1-4:11; Mark 1:2-13; Luke 3:1-23; 4:1-13; John 1:19-34
- ☐ 277 John 1:35-3:36
- ☐ 278 John 4; Matthew 4:12-17; Mark 1:14-15; Luke 4:14-30
- ☐ 279 Mark 1:16-45; Matthew 4:18-25; 8:2-4, 14-17; Luke 4:31-5:16
- ☐ 280 Matthew 9:1-17; Mark 2:1-22; Luke 5:17-39
- ☐ 281 John 5; Matthew 12:1-21; Mark 2:23-3:12; Luke 6:1-11
- ☐ 282 Matthew 5; Mark 3:13-19; Luke 6:12-36
- ☐ 283 Matthew 6-7; Luke 6:37-49
- ☐ 284 Luke 7; Matthew 8:1, 5-13; 11:2-30
- ☐ 285 Matthew 12:22-50; Mark 3:20-35; Luke 8:1-21
- ☐ 286 Mark 4:1-34; Matthew 13:1-53
- ☐ 287 Mark 4:35-5:43; Matthew 8:18, 23-34; 9:18-34; Luke 8:22-56
- ☐ 288 Mark 6:1-30; Matthew 13:54-58; 9:35-11:1; 14:1-12; Luke 9:1-10

Bible reading schedule

- ☐ 289 Matthew 14:13-36; Mark 6:31-56; Luke 9:11-17; John 6:1-21
- ☐ 290 John 6:22-7:1; Matthew 15:1-20; Mark 7:1-23
- ☐ 291 Matthew 15:21-16:20; Mark 7:24-8:30; Luke 9:18-21
- ☐ 292 Matthew 16:21-17:27; Mark 8:31-9:32; Luke 9:22-45
- ☐ 293 Matthew 18; 8:19-22; Mark 9:33-50; Luke 9:46-62; John 7:2-10
- ☐ 294 John 7:11-8:59
- ☐ 295 Luke 10:1-11:36
- ☐ 296 Luke 11:37-13:21
- ☐ 297 John 9-10
- ☐ 298 Luke 13:22-15:32
- ☐ 299 Luke 16:1-17:10; John 11:1-54
- ☐ 300 Luke 17:11-18:17; Matthew 19:1-15; Mark 10:1-16
- ☐ 301 Matthew 19:16-20:28; Mark 10:17-45; Luke 18:18-34
- ☐ 302 Matthew 20:29-34; 26:6-13; Mark 10:46-52; 14:3-9; Luke 18:35-19:28; John 11:55-12:11
- ☐ 303 Matthew 21:1-22; Mark 11:1-26; Luke 19:29-48; John 12:12-50
- ☐ 304 Matthew 21:23-22:14; Mark 11:27-12:12; Luke 20:1-19
- ☐ 305 Matthew 22:15-46; Mark 12:13-37; Luke 20:20-44
- ☐ 306 Matthew 23; Mark 12:38-44; Luke 20:45-21:4
- ☐ 307 Matthew 24:1-31; Mark 13:1-27; Luke 21:5-27
- ☐ 308 Matthew 24:32-26:5, 14-16; Mark 13:28-14:2, 10-11; Luke 21:28-22:6
- ☐ 309 Matthew 26:17-29; Mark 14:12-25; Luke 22:7-38; John 13
- ☐ 310 John 14-16
- ☐ 311 John 17:1-18:1; Matthew 26:30-46; Mark 14:26-42; Luke 22:39-46
- ☐ 312 Matthew 26:47-75; Mark 14:43-72; Luke 22:47-65; John 18:2-27
- ☐ 313 Matthew 27:1-26; Mark 15:1-15; Luke 22:66-23:25; John 18:28-19:16
- ☐ 314 Matthew 27:27-56; Mark 15:16-41; Luke 23:26-49; John 19:17-30
- ☐ 315 Matthew 27:57-28:8; Mark 15:42-16:8; Luke 23:50-24:12; John 19:31-20:10
- ☐ 316 Matthew 28:9-20; Mark 16:9-20; Luke 24:13-53; John 20:11-21:25
- ☐ 317 Acts 1-2
- ☐ 318 Acts 3-5
- ☐ 319 Acts 6:1-8:1
- ☐ 320 Acts 8:2-9:43
- ☐ 321 Acts 10-11
- ☐ 322 Acts 12-13
- ☐ 323 Acts 14-15
- ☐ 324 Galatians 1-3
- ☐ 325 Galatians 4-6
- ☐ 326 James
- ☐ 327 Acts 16:1-18:11
- ☐ 328 1 Thessalonians
- ☐ 329 2 Thessalonians; Acts 18:12-19:22
- ☐ 330 1 Corinthians 1-4
- ☐ 331 1 Corinthians 5-8
- ☐ 332 1 Corinthians 9-11
- ☐ 333 1 Corinthians 12-14
- ☐ 334 1 Corinthians 15-16
- ☐ 335 Acts 19:23-20:1; 2 Corinthians 1-4
- ☐ 336 2 Corinthians 5-9
- ☐ 337 2 Corinthians 10-13
- ☐ 338 Romans 1-3
- ☐ 339 Romans 4-6
- ☐ 340 Romans 7-8
- ☐ 341 Romans 9-11
- ☐ 342 Romans 12-15
- ☐ 343 Romans 16; Acts 20:2-21:16
- ☐ 344 Acts 21:17-23:35
- ☐ 345 Acts 24-26
- ☐ 346 Acts 27-28
- ☐ 347 Ephesians 1-3
- ☐ 348 Ephesians 4-6
- ☐ 349 Colossians
- ☐ 350 Philippians
- ☐ 351 Philemon; 1 Timothy 1-3
- ☐ 352 1 Timothy 4-6; Titus
- ☐ 353 2 Timothy
- ☐ 354 1 Peter
- ☐ 355 Jude; 2 Peter
- ☐ 356 Hebrews 1:1-5:10
- ☐ 357 Hebrews 5:11-9:28
- ☐ 358 Hebrews 10-11
- ☐ 359 Hebrews 12-13; 2 John; 3 John
- ☐ 360 1 John
- ☐ 361 Revelation 1-3
- ☐ 362 Revelation 4-9
- ☐ 363 Revelation 10-14
- ☐ 364 Revelation 15-18
- ☐ 365 Revelation 19-22

We take so much for granted every day—things like nature, food, and God's grace. Have you ever taken the time from running to school or sports practice to thank God for all He's provided for you? This week you'll have an opportunity to consider it!

prayer focus for this week

the Question — What is the writer saying?

the Answer — How can I apply this to my life?

sunday Psalm 104:1-13

Q Praising God's work and design on Earth

A Fix my eyes on His World and design.

Digging Deeper • Have you ever watched an accomplished painter as he worked on a canvas? It's amazing to watch how, with just a few strokes, a formless blob of paint becomes a beautiful landscape, complete with flowers, trees, birds, and a quiet lake. Today's passage gives us a glimpse of the Master Artist as He took the formless, empty canvas of His newly created earth (Genesis 1) and painted a masterpiece. Look around you—what do you see? Verse 13 says that the earth is satisfied with God's works. Are you satisfied with how He's created you? Remember that everything God created is a masterpiece, including you.
Instead of complaining about something that you wish you could change about yourself, stop right now and thank God for making you a work of art!

monday   Psalm 104:14-23

Q *How God designed us to his creation to live and survive.*

A *Rely on God's design and His works to live and glorify Him.*

Digging Deeper • Have you grumbled about a dinner your mom prepared recently? Do you wish you didn't have to share a room with your brother or sister? Have you ever wished you lived in a different neighborhood? All of us have probably been unsatisfied with circumstances in our lives at times. When you look at today's passage, you won't notice any hint of complaining. Each animal mentioned is portrayed as content with God's provision. Are you?
Is there a homeless shelter or another kind of service center near you? Contact them and volunteer to help serve once week for a month. Keep a journal of your thoughts and experiences. Share it with a youth leader.

tuesday   Psalm 104:24-35

Q *Rejoice in God's Creation*

A *Had vision or dream of Psalm. All heavenly creatures will be together on a new face of the earth. Sinners will vanish!*

Digging Deeper • Quick! What is something you do every second of every day without ever having to think about? It's something you are doing right now. In fact, if you stopped doing this thing, you would literally die. If you guessed *breathing*, congratulations! The psalmist, David was so grateful to God for providing his every breath that he desired to sing praises to the Lord as long as he could breathe (v. 33). More importantly, his prayer was that all he thought about would be pleasing to God.
Think through all the things you may take for granted (the world around you, food, shelter, health, life). Are there areas where you have not been thankful for all that God has provided for you? Name three ways you could begin to demonstrate a heart attitude like the one David expressed in this Psalm.

wednesday   Psalm 105:1-12

Q Seek God *AND PRAISE* and all His ways

A Everyday to remember him, Give thanks and praise. Seek HIT face.

Digging Deeper • To whom do you turn when you find yourself in trouble or discouraged? When plans don't turn out the way you wanted, how do you respond? Do you throw a pity party for yourself and sulk for a few days? Do you grumble and complain to anyone who will listen? How would your attitude be different if you followed what this psalm commands you to do—thank the Lord, call out to Him (v. 1), sing praises to Him (v. 2), spend time telling others about Him (v. 2), and glorify Him (v. 3)? When you think about all you have because you know Christ as your Savior, everything else may pale in comparison.

For the remainder of this week, make a daily list of five things you can praise God for. Challenge yourself to not repeat a single entry.

thursday   Psalm 105:13-25

Q He protected from getting my heart and emotions trampled on and sabotaged, destroyed by a man.

A Even when myself available for the Harm. The Lord God Almighty still *PROTECTED ME!*

Digging Deeper • Has someone who was much bigger and stronger than you ever challenged you to a fight? What did you do? If you were wise, perhaps you told your dad or older brother about it. You didn't want them to fight for you but rather just go with you as a source of support and strength. And when you showed up with your reinforcements, the presence of your dad or brother was probably enough to stop the fight. In the same way, God intervened for His children, the Israelites, throughout their history. Although they faced difficulties, He preserved them. If you are His child, you can be sure that He will preserve you and will be with you through every difficulty.

Spend time just looking for God. In what instances have you seen His protection? Keep a journal of these times so you won't forget.

friday Psalm 105:26-36

Digging Deeper • The attack on the World Trade Center in New York City on September 11, 2001 will forever be a part of U.S. and global history. Your grandchildren will probably study those dark hours someday because there are many lessons to be learned. Hopefully, if we learn well, tragedies like this won't happen again. But those who fail to learn are destined to repeat their mistakes. In today's passage, the Israelites needed to be reminded of God's faithfulness. Throughout the Old Testament, they are reminded repeatedly of all God did for them to bring them out of Egypt.

Are you living a life that demonstrates a grateful heart for the faithfulness of God? If not, how can you begin to live more for the Lord?

saturday Psalm 105:37-45

Not effectively communicating with my words and forming my thoughts and sentences to effectively convey what I feel and how I understand things.

To be grateful for where I am and how the Lord has taken care of me and Trust Him.

Digging Deeper • Your parents probably would never say this to you, but the reason they get upset when you complain about not getting those sneakers, CDs, or DVDs you want is because your heart is not satisfied or content with what they do provide for you. Sneakers come and go, CDs get scratched, and DVDs get lost or stolen, but the question remains: is your heart satisfied with what God provides for you through your parents? When you understand that all you have—where you live, the clothes you wear, and the food you enjoy—ultimately comes from God, you will not focus as much on what you don't have. Instead, an attitude of satisfaction and contentment will bring thanksgiving, blessing, joy, and gladness to you!

Name three things you have complained about in the last week. How could your reaction have been different?

Do you know how it feels to be taken for granted? Can you remember a time when you showed kindness to someone, and they didn't have the decency to say "thanks"? If you felt hurt and discouraged, imagine what it's like for the Lord. Ask God to use this week's study to develop a thankful heart within you!

prayer focus for this week

the Question   What is the writer saying?
the Answer   How can I apply this to my life?

sunday   Psalm 106:1-15

Digging Deeper • Have you ever wanted something so badly, you were willing to do anything to get it… perhaps even sin? Maybe it was that CD we spoke about yesterday. You may have been in the store and seen it on the shelf. You knew you didn't have the money with you, but you *really* wanted to have it, so you slipped it in your pocket and walked out of the store. At home, you snuck into your room to begin listening to it. How was the music? It wasn't as great as your friends said. Maybe it's good, but it could be the way you got it that made it less than satisfying. Your lust to have it caused you to sin, and that unsatisfied feeling is what is described in verse 15… a *leanness* in your soul.

Giving into the promise of temptation robs you of peace with God and yourself. Is it worth it?

monday Psalm 106:16-31

Digging Deeper • Is there someone you know at school or church that seems to have it all together? They may have a great personality or be popular, good-looking, a good student, President of the Class, or spiritually together. What is your reaction when you see him or her? Are you glad to see them and wish you could be like them? Or is your heart envious of them? Envy is discontentment on steroids! It demonstrates a heart of anger not only toward someone but also at God Himself because He did not make you like that person. Envy is always self-destructive; it can kill you (vv. 17-18, 29) and affect your relationship with God (vv. 19-21, 24-25). God wanted to destroy the Israelites because of their attitude (vv. 23, 26).
Imagine if God responded this way when you envy someone! Is there anyone that you are currently angry with? If so, how will you deal with it?

tuesday Psalm 106:32-48

Digging Deeper • When was the last time you disobeyed your parents? What were the results? There might have been an awkward silence, which may have seemed worse than any physical punishment you could endure. It's in these moments that the right thing to do is to humble yourself and go seek forgiveness. An attitude of sincere repentance usually results in mercy and restoration. Parents who see this type of attitude in their children should respond as God did with the Israelites (vv. 44-45). It may not stop you from suffering the consequences of your actions (Galatians 6:7), but you will be able to endure it, knowing that God and your parents love you!
Name three ways you can demonstrate a humble attitude toward your parents this week.

wednesday Psalm 107:1-16

Digging Deeper • Around the time when you were a wobbly two-year-old, you may have made your way into the kitchen where mom was cooking dinner. You noticed a nice, shiny pot, and you began reaching for its handle. Your mom cautioned you not to touch because it was hot. You had no idea what *hot* meant. All you knew was that you wanted it, so you grabbed the pot, spilling its contents. You soon understood what *hot* was, and that it wasn't good. Sometimes we only learn by being burned. Unfortunately, we often ignore warnings about sin, too, and as a result, we suffer. God allows it so that we learn and cry out to Him for help, and so we can make a habit of obeying Him and trusting what He says about the dangers of sin.
If you've been rescued from sin's grip, what do verses 2, 8, and 15 say we should do? Are you obeying?

thursday Psalm 107:17-32

Digging Deeper • Have you ever been caught in an unexpected storm? One minute the sun is shining and the sky is blue, and the next minute, the sun has run away and the clouds are black as midnight! It's not fun at all. If you are like most people, you seek the safest spot you can find for shelter. Life is like that sometimes—a car accident, a fire, a divorce, or the death of a parent can thrust you into what feels like a raging storm. Everywhere you turn, it seems like there is no place to run for safety. The good news is that if you know the Lord, He is with you and will bring you through whatever storm you are facing.
Is there someone you know who is going through a storm right now? Why not write them a note of encouragement using these verses to strengthen them?

friday   Psalm 107:33-43

Digging Deeper • Every event that happens in this world—every season, every flood or drought, every bounty of crops or famine, every president and world leader—everything is controlled and ordained by God Himself. What do you think about that? Are you willing to acknowledge that He is over all creation, and to understand that He makes no mistakes? Does that thought comfort you or anger you? These things are hard to remember sometimes, but it helps to put the right perspective on all that comes into your life, whether it be troubles or good things. Everything is under God's rule and authority. If you are wise, you'll know and understand it (v. 43). If you refuse to accept this, God has another name for you—a fool!

If you are wise, how will it impact how you respond to a crisis? What if you are a fool? How would you describe yourself now?

saturday   Psalm 108:1-13

Digging Deeper • You've been learning this week about God's control over every circumstance in your life. You've learned that sometimes you need to learn the hard way. You've discovered that admitting when you're wrong is the best response. And you've probably faced a rough storm sometime. Have you put into practice what God has been trying to teach you? Have you become wise or remained a fool? Is your heart like David's—fixed and laser-focused on God and what He is doing? Have you praised Him through the difficulties, and praised Him for those trials as well? Have you testified about His goodness? Verse 13 in today's passage says that through God we shall do valiantly, or have victory.

List three of the victories God has enabled you to have this week over your enemies (sin). Share them with your youth leader.

One thing that is so great about the Word of God is how it does not pretend that Christians are perfect. You could say that those mentioned in Scripture are shown "warts and all." They struggled with the same issues you do—anger, hurt, pain, depression, and fear. Watch this week to see how God's people handle difficulties.

prayer focus for this week

the **Question** — What is the writer saying?

the **Answer** — How can I apply this to my life?

sunday   Psalm 109:1-10

Digging Deeper • Is it always wrong to get angry? Not necessarily. As in the case of today's passage, David was rightly upset because he was being falsely accused and slandered. Notice that he did not try to prove his innocence by attacking his accusers. Rather, he did what the Lord would want us to do—he turned to God and trusted Him to take care of his enemies. While it was frustrating to have even his good spoken of as evil, he maintained a good testimony before his accusers, offering love. Christ Himself treated His accusers the same way.

How should you respond when falsely accused? Can you see the difference between righteous anger and unrighteous anger? Do you react personally to those who attack, or do you pray like David? How would the Lord want you to respond?

monday Psalm 109:11-20

Digging Deeper • Does it seem to you that living life on the edge is somehow more exciting than trying to obey the Lord? Television and the movies show the glories of this type of lifestyle without revealing its ultimate end. God's Word has a different picture of the destiny of a man who chooses to live apart from God's control. He'll get no favor, no mercy, and no hope of forgiveness once he dies. This psalm says he will wear cursing like a garment. This is a picture of a desperate man! Don't envy those who live this lifestyle. Instead, pray for them and try to find opportunities to share Christ.

Make a list of three friends you know at school who need Christ. Pray for them daily for the next month, asking God to give you a witnessing opportunity.

tuesday Psalm 109:21-31

Digging Deeper • We all get down and feel discouraged sometimes. Maybe you've felt like David, when it seemed everyone was against him. It sounds as if he is very discouraged in today's passage. It seemed like his prayers were not getting answered—at least not as quickly as he wanted. Instead of allowing depression to grip his soul, though, he turned to the Lord and cried for help. He knew he could trust God's character and His love for His children. In the midst of the problems he faced, David praised God.

When you are frustrated and hurting inside, how can prayer and praising God help you? How can you help a friend who is struggling right now? Maybe they could use an encouraging phone call today.

wednesday Psalm 110:1-7

Digging Deeper • Who do you say that Jesus is? To some, He was just a good man. But a good man does not claim to be God. For others, He was just a prophet. But a prophet does not accept worship from anyone. Jesus was the Messiah, the Savior of the world, and He offered Himself on the cross for your sins. The first time He came, it was as the Lamb of God Who takes away the sins of men. Now He sits in Heaven, waiting for the time to return for His own children. When He returns, He will come as the Lion of Judah to judge His enemies.

Which side are you on? Will you meet Him as Savior or Judge? There is no time to wait – He could return at any moment.

thursday Psalm 111:1-10

Digging Deeper • What are your educational plans? Do you hope to graduate one day with a degree in nuclear physics? Do you want to teach at a university? Do you want to become the next Bill Gates? It's great to have goals and plans, but remember that it is possible to be intellectually smart but remain spiritually foolish. These verses talk about fearing God—acknowledging and understanding that He is the source of all knowledge and wisdom. He and His Word should be where you turn first for answers in life. He is the only One who can make sense out of this life and its problems. His ways are perfect.

Do your future plans begin with obeying Christ and His Word? Is your goal to please Him in all things, including your job and other big decisions?

friday Psalm 112:1-10

Digging Deeper • When detectives begin looking for a suspect of a crime, they often turn to a profiler who can give them clues to a person's characteristics, behaviors, and habits, simply by looking at the evidence the detectives have gathered. It's amazing how they are able to do it. Today's verses outline for you the profile of a person who *fears the Lord*. These are essentials for a God-fearing person, while other things, such as monetary wealth, are not necessarily guarantees. **See if you can underline each of the characteristics in these verses. How does your life match up to what God calls the person who "fears Him"? As you fear God and are obedient to God and His Word, you will begin to resemble this profile.**

saturday Psalm 113:1-9

Digging Deeper • What do you do when you see a homeless person on the street? What about that kid in school who doesn't wear the newest clothes? Some people respond by turning away and ignoring the poor person or mocking that kid at school. If you fear the Lord, you understand that there is no room for these attitudes. In God's eyes, all men are valuable and have dignity because they are made in His image. He controls who is poor or rich and what position of authority they hold. God's grace is the only thing who makes you who you are. **Instead of boasting, spend time praising God for His grace. Think of practical ways you can help a homeless person or someone else in need, maybe by serving at a soup kitchen or a shelter. Demonstrate Christ's love to the world around you.**

Week 4

Are you ready for an extreme makeover? We all have our ideas about how we would like to look, but God has His own plans for us. At the end of this week's Quiet Time, the new you will be revealed. Who will you look like after God does an extreme makeover on you?

prayer focus for this week

the Question   What is the writer saying?
the Answer   How can I apply this to my life?

sunday   2 Corinthians 1:1-11

Digging Deeper • "Why are you doing this to me, God?" If you have not asked God this question yet, you probably will. Today we start the book of 2 Corinthians. Paul knew a lot about trouble (Acts 19:23-20:3), and he knew that God always had a purpose in it. God comforts us so that we can comfort others (v. 4). We have trouble so we can encourage someone else who is having a hard time (v. 6). There's a saying, "God never wastes a hurt." As God brings you through the trouble you are having, you will soon discover others who are also having trouble, and you can be an encouragement to them.

Has God already delivered you from trouble? How did He do it? Look for someone today that is struggling. Encourage that person just as God has encouraged you.

monday 2 Corinthians 1:12-24

Digging Deeper • Have you ever been falsely accused? Paul had written the book of 1 Corinthians to the church in Corinth one year before, and now he was writing his follow-up letter. He talks about his conscience being honest before the people (v. 12). He had rebuked the church for sin that was allowed to continue; now he was sharing his joy for them (v. 14). Paul had to defend his truthfulness in verses 15-20 by saying that his actions and words had been reliable, just as all the promises of God would be fulfilled in Jesus Christ. Paul was honest before God the Father, Son, and Holy Spirit (vv. 21-24) and viewed himself as a fellow helper to the Corinthian believers.
What do you think Paul thought about God? What do you think he thought about himself? What do you think he thought about other people? How would you answer these questions about yourself?

tuesday 2 Corinthians 2:1-13

Digging Deeper • False teachers had lied about Paul to the church in Corinth. Now Paul tells the church why he had not come back to see them. His love for them caused him to stay away so that they would have a chance to correct the sin in the church. This love motivated Paul (vv. 1-4). In verses 5-11, Paul tells them to forgive the man who had sinned (1 Corinthians 5) and to restore him to fellowship. Once we ask God and fellow Christians for forgiveness, we have to forgive that person. Paul is also showing his need for Christian fellowship (vv. 12-13)—he needed encouragement from Titus, and he went looking for him.
Have you forgiven someone who has sinned against you? How many reasons for forgiveness can you find in today's verses?

wednesday 2 Corinthians 2:14 - 3:5

Digging Deeper • Paul is discouraged, but in his discouragement he sees himself in a great triumphant procession (v. 14). Jesus Christ is the Great General who is leading Paul. Paul is following God, and he is telling the truth to lost and saved people (vv. 15-17). People were important to Paul (vv. 1-5); what these people were in Christ was the proof of Paul's ministry. These people had been changed, and their lives were proof that Paul was teaching the truth. It was not Paul who was adequate within himself, but Christ who made him adequate to do God's will (compare 2:16 with 3:5).

Are you discouraged today? Ask God to allow you to view yourself in the great victory procession Paul describes here. Do you feel you cannot succeed in the Christian life? Be sure you are trusting in God alone.

thursday 2 Corinthians 3:6-18

Digging Deeper • Do you understand the New Testament (v. 6) and the Old Testament (v. 14)? Paul tells us that the Old Testament law brought only death, and the New Testament (new covenant) brought life. But the false teachers in Corinth were teaching legalism—they wanted people to live by a list of rules. The new covenant is based on living life in the power of the Holy Spirit and becoming just like Jesus Christ. Paul had become a minister of the new covenant; he was living his life in the power and liberty found in Jesus Christ.

Are you becoming more and more like Jesus every day (v. 18)? Do you live your life by rules, or are you allowing the Holy Spirit and the Word of God to transform you into the person that God wants you to be?

friday 2 Corinthians 4:1-7

Digging Deeper • Every Christian is called into ministry. Paul's special ministry always amazed him. He never got over the fact that he had received mercy from God. Like Paul, we are just servants preaching and teaching Jesus Christ to people who are lost and blind. Thus every Christian who ministers must live a pure life and have a clear conscience. God has shined His light into our hearts, and it is this light—His glory in us—that is truly amazing. Paul says that we are just clay pots (v. 7), and the real treasure inside us is Jesus Christ and His Gospel. No one really notices the clay pot when Jesus is shining out.

What are you doing this week to let the light of the Gospel shine out of your life to others? How do you resemble a clay pot? How would you describe the glory and life of Jesus Christ?

saturday 2 Corinthians 4:8-18

Digging Deeper • We all like to be happy as we serve the Lord. Paul has spent a lot of time in the previous verses talking about "the glory of God" (4:6) and how we are changed into looking just like Jesus "from glory to glory" (3:18). Now, Paul tells us that suffering for Jesus Christ is a big part of bringing glory to God. One of the keys to understanding why God allows trouble in our lives is found in verse 11: "that the life also of Jesus might be made manifest [revealed] in our mortal flesh." Paul tells us to look on the things that are eternal. There is more to life than just what happens to us on the outside.

List the troubles that you have today. Now list what God has done for you already through salvation, and what He will do for you throughout all eternity. Can you see how God is using you for His glory?

Week 5

Who is your hero? Whom do you want to be like? Paul wanted to be just like Jesus, and because of that, we should be happy to follow Paul as he followed Christ. Paul's genuine love for Christ and others is revealed in this week's Quiet Time.

prayer focus for this week

the Question   What is the writer saying?

the Answer   How can I apply this to my life?

sunday   2 Corinthians 5:1-10

Digging Deeper • Do you ever wonder what will happen to you when you die? Paul was not afraid to die. In fact, he really wanted to be in Heaven with the Lord. Paul had complete confidence in God that, at the very moment he was absent from the body (when he died), he would be present with the Lord. Paul had a godly ambition also. Verse 9 speaks of our ambition being "to be well pleasing to Him." This is the most noble of all ambitions! Paul lived each moment knowing that he would one day appear before the Judgment Seat of Christ.

Ask God today to make Heaven as real to you as it was to Paul. Is your greatest ambition to please Christ? Are you living today with the Judgment Seat of Christ in mind?

monday 2 Corinthians 5:11-21

Digging Deeper • What is your greatest ambition? Paul already told us that his greatest ambition was to please Christ (v. 9). Now, Paul pours on the reasons for serving Christ. One motive was the terror of the Lord (v. 11), knowing that God would judge the Christian. The love of Christ motivated Paul in verse 14. He knew that God had given him the ministry of reconciliation and the word of reconciliation (vv. 18-19). He knew that he was an "ambassador for Christ," and his job was to urge men to come to God. Because Jesus took our sin upon Himself, we are made righteous before God.

Can you see that God has called you to be an ambassador like He called Paul? Will you tell someone about how he can be reconciled to God today? Will you let the love of Christ motivate you so you share this with others?

tuesday 2 Corinthians 6:1-10

Digging Deeper • Has anyone ever given you a job to do and instructions on how to do it? Sometimes instructions just involve doing as you are told, and sometimes they get very specific. Some instructions sound like fun, but often they do not describe the dirty work involved. Paul gives us a summary of his instructions in these verses today. He describes his job as working together with God—he was to urge men to be saved but was not to offend others. He had to approve himself as a minister of God in over twenty areas. Circle the words *in*, *by*, and *as* to see these areas.

Are you ready for instructions that matter? List the areas in which you would have difficulty following God's instructions, and areas where it may be easier. Will you follow these instructions?

wednesday 2 Corinthians 6:11-7:1

Digging Deeper • When love (5:14) is your motivation, then separation becomes natural. When you have a wife or a husband, you become separate from every other person on the planet in order to love your spouse exclusively. Paul's great love for Christ caused him to be separated from everything that was contrary to the mind of God (vv. 11-16a). Then Paul concluded that he was to be separated to God Himself (vv. 16b-7:1). Because of Paul's love for Christ, he couldn't think of doing anything to compromise his deep love for Him.

Are you having trouble giving up some relationship or habit that is contrary to the heart and mind of God? Will you resolve today to love God Himself above anything on earth? What are you willing to give up in order to enjoy unbroken fellowship with Jesus Christ?

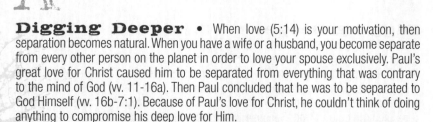

thursday 2 Corinthians 7:2-16

Digging Deeper • Are you a *real* person? Paul demonstrates his true heart of love for the Corinthians in this passage. He admits being fearful and depressed. He tells the Corinthians that he needed people (Titus) to encourage him. Paul was rejoicing that the Corinthians had repented of their sins after his first letter and had gone on to live out their faith with great zeal. He concludes by saying that he has confidence in them in all things. Every person needs to be loved, and every person wants to be valued for who he is.

Is there someone in your life today that needs to hear you say "I love you"? Who needs to hear you say "I am proud of you" today? When we love people and value them, we should tell them, just like Paul did.

friday 2 Corinthians 8:1-15

Digging Deeper • When you are in love, sometimes you do things that seem silly. Giving gifts to the one you love can sometimes get out of hand, but this is the nature of love. Love gives, and John 3:16 proves that point when it tells us that "God so loved the world that He gave." Our giving in the church is no different. Paul tells about the Macedonians, who first gave themselves to the Lord and then graciously and joyously insisted on giving an offering to the Lord Jesus Christ (v. 8)! This is the greatest example of giving. Look how the words of *love*, *faith*, *sincerity*, *joy*, *willingness*, and *grace* characterized their giving.

Have you become joyful and gracious in your giving? How can the example of Christ giving His life for us motivate us to be faithful in our tithes and offerings? Can you trust God with your money?

saturday 2 Corinthians 8:16-24

Digging Deeper • Paul was handling the generous offering of the believers in Corinth with absolute integrity. Because of their deep love for Christ and Paul, the offering would be large (v. 14 talks about "their abundance" when it comes to their giving), and so Paul sent Titus and "the brother" (v. 18) who was not named. This brother and Titus were "messengers of the churches, and the glory of Christ" (v. 23), so you know they could be trusted. Any offering in the church given for the Lord's work should be handled in an honest way. When it was time to give the offering that was promised, the church could have complete confidence that it would be used properly.

Have you made a promise on which you need to follow through? Are you handling your money in a way that is honoring to God?

Week 6

Great warriors and great athletes often must put it all on the line as they approach the finish line. At that point, what they have done in training and who they really are makes the difference in winning and losing. Watch the great warrior and athlete, the Apostle Paul, win in your Quiet Time this week!

prayer focus for this week

the**Question**   **What is the writer saying?**

the**Answer**   **How can I apply this to my life?**

sunday   2 Corinthians 9:1-15

Digging Deeper • Have you ever heard the question "What would you do if you knew you could not fail?" Paul's promise in chapter 9 about giving is fail-proof. He tells us that we should always be ready to give (vv. 1-5). We should give generously (vv. 6-11a), because God is able to give us more than we ever give Him. Verse 7 says we should give cheerfully because God loves a cheerful giver. God has promised to pour out His love on the person who gives cheerfully. Finally, thankfulness is always a part of Christian giving (vv. 11b-15), and the greatest gift of all is Jesus Christ. He is God's unspeakable gift and the reason that we can be cheerful givers. **Are you a cheerful giver? Have you taken God up on His promise that He is able to make all grace abound toward you? Make a point to give cheerfully.**

monday   2 Corinthians 10:1-18

Digging Deeper • Paul is on a rescue mission to save the Christians at Corinth from false teachers who are trying to discredit Paul's ministry. Verses 4-5 should be memorized by every Christian who wants to win spiritual battles. Paul knew that spiritual battles are fought in the mind and will be won with the Word of God. He was ready to fight false doctrine and win back the church he helped establish. Paul was a real man of God and had the credentials to prove it, but he knew to expect a battle because Satan is never prepared to relinquish anything without a fight!
What are you ready to fight for? Paul obviously loved God, people, and the truth of God's Word. Check your life and see what you are willing to fight to defend. What will you do if someone makes fun of the Bible, uses God's name in vain, or refuses to listen to your witness?

tuesday   2 Corinthians 11:1-15

Digging Deeper • Paul loved his converts at Corinth, but Satan had come into the church and was trying to steal the bride of Christ out of it. The supposedly new apostles or false teachers who have come into the church (v. 4) are teaching another Jesus, are led by a false spirit, and are teaching a different gospel. Paul declares his love (v. 11) and warns them that these false apostles (vv. 13-15) look like the real thing but in fact are following Satan and will ultimately be destroyed. Real discernment will be needed, and the best way to determine the true from the false is to compare these people's teachings with the Word of God.
To whom are you listening, and what are you reading? Do your favorite Christian authors pass the test of Scripture? What are they teaching about Jesus Christ, the Holy Spirit, and the Bible?

Wednesday 2 Corinthians 11:16-33

Digging Deeper • We all know about Hollywood actors. On the screen they play the part of a different person, but in real life they are just themselves. Paul is no actor—he is a real apostle, and he lists what he has done in real life to prove it. The false apostles that Paul is fighting are the actors. Look at Paul's resume of suffering. Hardly anyone could rival what Paul went through for the Gospel, for Jesus, and for the Christians to whom he ministered. Listen to Paul share his heartfelt love for the Corinthian believers. Paul's steadfastness in the face of extreme adversity should encourage every Christian to keep on keeping on for Jesus!

Are you afraid to suffer for Jesus Christ? What will it take for you to turn back from serving Christ? Why not write out your commitment to Christ, telling Him that you are willing to follow Him no matter the cost?

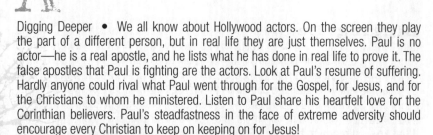

Thursday 2 Corinthians 12:1-10

Digging Deeper • If you go to certain areas of the Pentagon, you must have security clearance in order to hear the greatest secrets of our government. Paul was granted top security clearance by God and ushered into the third Heaven, where he heard "unspeakable words." He is talking about how God inspired him to write Scripture. Because of this great privilege, God also gave him "a thorn in the flesh," apparently some physical sickness or affliction, to be sure he always remained humble. Paul's "thorn" was not removed, but God gave him the grace to glory in it so he could have the power of God on his life.

How are you viewing your various troubles (v. 10)? How will you prepare to live with troubles, knowing God will give you grace to live with them for His glory, in order to have God's power in your life?

friday   2 Corinthians 12:11-21

Digging Deeper • Whom can you trust in life? Paul tells us that he is trustworthy, and his life and credentials as an apostle cannot be disputed. Comparing Scripture with Scripture throughout the New Testament, we see the uniqueness of the office of apostle that Paul fulfilled. Now that the canon (writings) of Scripture is complete, the office is no longer in existence. Finally, Paul uses strong warnings to the church, based on his apostles' office (v. 11), his love for the Corinthians (v. 15), and his desire to build them up (v. 19). He challenges them to clean up the sin that had been allowed to run through the church.

Whom can you edify (encourage) in their walk with Christ this week? Be sure to make an appointment to talk with them heart-to-heart about the things that matter most to God.

saturday   2 Corinthians 13:1-14

Digging Deeper • Everyone who goes to school eventually has to take a test. Paul has finished his second letter to the Corinthians. He has been a faithful teacher; he has the proper balance of love and sternness. They know he has taught them the truth. Now they must take the test to see if they are true Christians. "Examine yourselves whether you be in the faith," he says. He wants them to look into their hearts and see that they really are true believers in Christ. Paul wants them to be assured of their salvation and be perfect (mature) in their walk with Christ.

What about you? When you examine yourself, do you find that you are a true believer? Have you repented of your sin and put your complete trust in Christ alone for your salvation? How will your life be changed after your study of 2 Corinthians?

This week, pay attention and try to hear God's voice speaking to you through His Word. See how He guides people to make the right choices and what happens when they refuse to listen. Don't make the same mistake!

prayer focus for this week

the Question — What is the writer saying?

the Answer — How can I apply this to my life?

sunday 1 Samuel 1:1-18

Q

A

Digging Deeper • How do you feel when you are falsely accused of doing wrong? Are you quick to make judgments based on the actions of another person, before getting all the facts? We are all prone to do that, but it can cause problems between you and that other person. Instead of jumping to conclusions, the biblical thing to do is to ask questions and get the whole story. If Eli had only been sensitive to Hannah's situation and asked some questions, he might have avoided falsely accusing her. The next time you are tempted to make a judgment based on how the circumstances appear, remember to ask questions of those involved.
Is there a situation where you did not get all the facts before making a judgment? Is there someone you need to reconcile with because of a false accusation or misunderstanding? Get it right today!

monday 1 Samuel 1:19 — 2:11

Digging Deeper • Have you ever begged your parents for a puppy, promising to take care of it every day and feed and clean it? Did you follow through on the promise? Did your parents hold you to it, even on the coldest mornings? One thing you probably learned was that you should have been more careful making promises. Sometimes promises cost you more than you really intended. In yesterday's passage, Hannah prayed for a son, promising to give him back to God forever. Today, we learn that God granted her request by blessing her with a child, but He also expected her to keep her promise. Keeping promises may be difficult, but it is necessary, especially to God!

Can you identify a promise you made to God but have not kept? What should you do about it? What will you do about it? When will you do it?

tuesday 1 Samuel 3:1-21

Digging Deeper • Wouldn't it be cool if you could hear God speaking to you directly? Would you recognize His voice? What if He told you He was going to judge someone close to you? Would you keep the bad news to yourself or share it with that person? While you won't actually hear God's audible voice, God still speaks to you through His Word. Are you listening? Are you obeying His commands? You may be thinking of someone right now that needs to hear of God's love and respond to it rather than face His wrath for neglecting to hear. Will you tell them?

Do you have a friend or relative that is facing God's judgment because they don't know Him? What message should you bring them? Are you willing to be used by Him to help change their life by sharing the Gospel? When?

wednesday 1 Samuel 6:1-15

Digging Deeper • How do you make decisions about important issues? To whom do you turn? Do you trust your instincts or circumstances only? Be careful of the danger of trusting circumstances in making your decision, because they may not lead you to the right one. It's vital that you first seek the Lord through prayer and look for the wisdom He gives through His Word. Ask Him for guidance and direction. Also seek out individuals who can help. Your parents, youth leaders, or other wise and mature individuals can help guide you in making decisions that please God. There is wisdom in seeking the help and counsel of mature believers.

What is the toughest decision you've made lately? How did you decide what to do? Develop a list of three godly individuals who can help you make important decisions. Ask them if they would help you when needed.

thursday 1 Samuel 7:1-17

Digging Deeper • What do you think of when you hear the word *idol*? Most people think about a carved image that people worship. In reality, an idol is anyone or anything that takes first place in your life or controls you. In other words, an idol is whatever is more important than God in your life. Idols in our life are those things that we devote our attention, time, passion, and money towards. They can come in the form of things, people, and even actions, such as talking or chatting online, listening to music, or even watching TV. Ask yourself, how important are these areas to me compared to spending time with God? Samuel urged the Israelites to put away their idols and serve God only.

In the next five days, keep track of idols that keep you from spending time with God or serving Him. Ask God for strength to prioritize your life.

friday 1 Samuel 8:1-22

Digging Deeper • Are you the type of person who refuses to listen to advice, especially from your parents or an older adult? You may dismiss them (thinking they are just old-fashioned) only to find out later that they were right. What you might not realize is that they might have made a similar mistake when they were young and learned the hard way. You could save yourself pain and trouble if you would trust them! God sees things so much clearer than we do; He knows where a decision you make will lead you. The Israelites lived to regret their decision not to follow God because they wanted their own way. Don't make the same mistake!

Are you like the Israelites, who refused to listen? Where might this stubbornness lead you? How can you avoid it?

saturday 1 Samuel 9:1-3, 15-27

Digging Deeper • Wouldn't it be great if God personally revealed His plan for your life to you? How would you respond? Would you be scared? Imagine if He told you it was to become president of your country? As someone who might not even be out of high school yet, it would seem impossible. God probably won't literally speak to you, but He does have a plan for your life. Do you want to know it? Are you scared? Don't be! Remain faithful and obedient to Him and allow Him to guide you through His Word. If you will trust Him, you might be surprised by what He has in store for you! Remember to keep moving forward for God. Just like a car, it's easier for Him to direct you if you're moving rather than standing still.

Are you willing to trust God with your future? How can staying in His Word help you to know His will? What have you learned this week?

Are you a people-pleaser or a God-pleaser? We all want to have an impact on our world, and our friends make a big difference in what impact we make. See if you can discover how much influence others have on you as you study King Saul's life!

prayer focus for this week

the Question
What is the writer saying?

the Answer
How can I apply this to my life?

sunday 1 Samuel 10:1-10, 17-19

Digging Deeper • Sometimes change is slow and gradual, like the physical changes that happen as you grow into adulthood. But it's different when God makes a change in your life; the things you used to do, you don't do them anymore! Just as God changed Saul's heart, when you meet Christ, He also changes your heart. That means there should be a change of desire, focus, attitude, and goals. You should no longer live to please yourself, but God! Saul's family and friends couldn't believe the change in him (vv. 11-18), but they couldn't deny it, either. God had given him a different heart toward the things of God.

Can people see the change God has made in your life? If so, praise God! If not, why not? Has there truly been a change? If you're not sure, speak to your youth leader or your pastor today.

monday   1 Samuel 12:1-5, 13-25

Digging Deeper • Do you know people who consistently disobey their parents, even if they are warned of the consequences repeatedly? How do they react when they realize they are finally about to be punished? Up until that moment, they acted like they didn't care about it, but now they are crying and pleading for mercy! It's tough to feel pity for them because you saw it coming. If only they had listened and reconsidered their actions, the outcome would have been different. The Israelites learned the hard way, by suffering the consequences. How about you? Are you stubborn when it comes to listening to warnings? Even if you've had to learn the hard way, God calls you to repent and follow Him (vv. 20, 24).
Have you suffered the consequences of refusing to listen? How can you serve God in spite of it? It's not too late to have a change of heart.

tuesday   1 Samuel 13:1-14

Digging Deeper • Are you an impatient person? Have you ever secretly opened your birthday or Christmas presents before it was time and then re-wrapped them? Besides spoiling the surprise, were you disappointed? Not willing to wait for the right time can ruin so many things. Hundreds of young people unwrap the precious gift of sex before God's appointed time (marriage) and suffer the consequences the rest of their lives (unwanted pregnancies, guilt, sexually transmitted diseases, etc.). Obeying God's Word always results in blessings. Because of Saul's impatience, he sinned and it resulted in the kingdom being ripped away from him and given to another. Impatient choices usually result in negative consequences.
What consequences are you suffering because of your impatience? What steps can you take to avoid them in the future?

wednesday   1 Samuel 14:47 - 15:11

Digging Deeper • Stop what you are doing right now and go ask your parents, "When is the time I bring you the most joy?" They will probably say that it is when you listen to them and obey them. The same is true about your heavenly Father. Nothing grieves God more than someone who doesn't obey Him, or worse, when they only partially obey Him. Can't you imagine God asking, "What part of 'thou shall not' didn't you understand?" Partial obedience is complete disobedience, and God cannot bless you. God's commands are not to make your life difficult—they are for your good; He knows what's best for you! Do you believe that? Do your actions show it?

Are you willing to obey Jesus whether others do or not? Find another Christian friend who wants to do the same and encourage each other.

thursday   1 Samuel 15:12-29

Digging Deeper • One thing that most people fear and dislike is being humiliated or made fun of by others. When you fear people and what they think more than you fear God, it leads to trouble. You will do things that you know you shouldn't to get their approval, such as drinking or smoking, using foul language, listening to suggestive jokes, or cheating on tests. You could justify your actions by saying it's necessary to be like them in order to win them to Christ. But God never desires that you sin just to be a witness to others. Obedience to His Word is more important than sacrificing your testimony!

Have you been pleasing people rather than pleasing God? How would obeying God help you to be a better witness for Him?

friday 1 Samuel 16:1, 6-23

Digging Deeper • When God went looking for a replacement for Saul, He didn't choose the strongest or the tallest man—human power and ability had little to do with His choice. He needed a man of character whose heart's desire was to please God, because this man was going to lead and influence the nation for years. When it comes to choosing friends, you need to be just as selective, because your friends will influence you. Friends will either draw you closer to God or pull you away from Him. By choosing friends who have good character and want to please God, you will increase your ability to make wise choices.

Do you sense a desire to please God in the friends you choose? Do they make wise decisions that agree with God's Word? Are they rebellious toward authority? How can prayer help you to choose friends more wisely?

saturday 1 Samuel 17:1-16

Digging Deeper • Are you intimidated by people who are older or bigger than you? For example, that first day as a freshman in high school can be very scary, especially if you don't know anyone. Seniors seem like giants to freshmen, and some take great pleasure in teasing and taunting others because of their size. If you are ever in a situation like this, remember that God is bigger than the person who is causing trouble. Trust that He can protect you, and don't do anything that will bring shame on Him or ruin your testimony. Look at Philippians 4:6-7. How does God want you to handle trouble? God is bigger and stronger than any problem or person that is causing you trouble.

What will happen to you if you allow yourself to give into your fears? How can prayer help you in the trouble you are facing right now?

This week you will learn how people react in troublesome times. You can rest assured that there's something for you to learn. How you react when trouble comes reveals a great deal about your character! Ask God to teach you to respond to trouble in a way that pleases Him.

prayer focus for this week

the Question What is the writer saying?

the Answer How can I apply this to my life?

sunday 1 Samuel 17:17-30

Q

A

Digging Deeper • Trying to do the right thing can cause others to think you are showing off. How people respond can be an indication of what is really going on in their hearts. There is a direct connection between the heart and the tongue. Under normal conditions, people can control what they say and how they talk to others; however, the true test comes when they are upset. It's when the pressure comes that their hearts are exposed. They may launch word bombs at you that are meant to hurt you deeply. The way that you respond in those situations also proves the condition of your heart. If you desire to please God, you won't respond in anger, but in kindness, just as Christ would (1 Peter 2:21-23).

Take note of how many times you get upset today and how you responded. Does it show that you wanted your way or God's way?

monday 1 Samuel 17:31-47

Digging Deeper • Are you going through a hard time right now? Would you say that you are doing all right under the circumstances? No matter what's happening, God wants you to be above your circumstances. Maybe you need to get together with a close friend or youth leader who can help you see God's faithfulness. Perhaps you need to remember that God is in control of all things, including your problem. His desire is that you trust Him to see you through. No matter how big the giant is, God will help you defeat it, if you will use the weapons He's given you—His Word, prayer, and faith. These weapons are sufficient to help you!
Are you growing in your trust and faith in Christ through the difficulties you are facing? Write the name of someone who can help you keep a God-centered perspective on the problem. Do you need to call someone now?

tuesday 1 Samuel 17:48-58

Digging Deeper • Do you try to avoid problems by running away or ignoring them? Guess what? They don't go away on their own! The best thing to do is face them head-on like David did. He applied the fighting skills he learned as a shepherd to defeat his enemy. You probably will never have to fight a bear or a lion, but hopefully as you study God's Word, you'll learn some fighting skills that will help you defeat the enemy. If you will stand firm in God's power, He will give you the victory and you will encourage others to fight, too (v. 52)!
What have you been learning about God and His Word that will help you defeat the enemy? Who has encouraged you to fight the enemy by their example? Who are you encouraging by your example?

wednesday 1 Samuel 18:1-16

Digging Deeper • Picture this: you and your best friend are both trying out for the lead part in the school play. He gets the part; you get the same part, but as the understudy. How do you feel? Are you (a) genuinely happy he got the part, (b) outwardly happy but secretly praying he gets sick on opening night so you can show everyone how it was supposed to be done, or (c) so upset that you quit the play and stop being friends with him. If you picked either (b) or (c), maybe you have a problem with jealousy. Look at where jealousy can lead if you allow it to consume you (vv. 10-11). If you find that others are jealous of you, be sure that you follow David's example in verse 14.
Have you allowed jealousy to destroy your relationship with someone? Ask God and the other person to forgive you. Do it today!

thursday 1 Samuel 19:1-18

Digging Deeper • Do you have a friend who is always looking out for you? Does he or she warn you if they see you heading for trouble? Do they defend you when you are verbally or physically attacked? Do they speak well of you to others when you are not around? If so, you need to thank God for them. God has blessed you with an incredible friend. Do all you can to preserve that friendship. Are you the same kind of friend to others? If you want friends like the one described, you need to be that kind of friend to others!
Are you willing to put the needs and concerns of your friends above your own? Can they count on you when they are in trouble? Do you love them enough to confront them when they are wrong?

friday 1 Samuel 20:1-23

Digging Deeper • When you have to make an important decision, the source you use to get your advice from makes all the difference. For example, if you had car trouble, you wouldn't call a surgeon for advice; for a toothache you wouldn't consult a lawyer. Hopefully you would choose someone with insight and experience in that particular field. You want someone who will give you a correct evaluation of the problem, who will be honest with you and offer a solution. Jonathan loved David, and David knew he could count on Jonathan for wise advice, honesty, and a solution to the problem he had with King Saul.

Can your friends count on you to give them wise advice with complete honesty (even when they are wrong!), and a workable solution to the problems they face? Can you count on them to do the same?

saturday 1 Samuel 20:24-42

Digging Deeper • Have you ever gotten upset because a mutual friend supported someone else's point of view instead of yours? Because your pride was hurt, you might have become angry, and it strained your relationship with that friend. Being angry can cause a lot of damage—emotionally, physically, and spiritually—both to you and the other person. Look what happened to Saul. He thought evil of David (v. 26) and became abusive toward others (v. 30). He allowed his emotions to rule his actions (v. 33), and it destroyed his relationship with his own son, Jonathan (v. 34). He died a pitiful, broken man. Was it worth it? Don't let pride cause you to respond sinfully.

Is there someone with whom you are angry? How is it affecting you in the areas mentioned above? What needs to change in your life and attitude?

Week 10

A lot can happen in 40 years. Did you ever consider what might happen to you in the next 40 years of your life? David probably would have never imagined how the decisions he made as a teenager would follow him all his life, and how abandoning his convictions would hurt his heart at the end.

prayer focus for this week

the Question — What is the writer saying?

the Answer — How can I apply this to my life?

sunday   2 Samuel 5:1-10

Q

A

Digging Deeper • Saul has died, and now his kingdom would be passed on to someone else. David happened to be that someone else, but he had to wait 12 years after he was anointed king to actually be crowned king. Then he had to wait another seven years before he was king of the whole nation. His patience paid off, and we are told he grew greatly because God was with him. He eventually reigned for 40 years altogether. This should teach us to never give up, and to keep following the Lord—we will see God's hand of blessing on our lives.

Are you tired of waiting on the Lord for His perfect timing in your life? Don't lose heart; God knows exactly where you are today. What great work do you think that God is preparing you for?

monday 2 Samuel 9:1-13

Digging Deeper • The story of David and Mephibosheth in this chapter is one of the most beautiful pictures of grace in the Bible. David remembered the promise he made as a teenager to his teenage friend, Jonathan (1 Samuel 20:15). Now as king at 30 plus years of age, he lavishly pours out love to the son of his friend. We too have received life through the grace of the King, Who sought us and became our Savior.
Who do you need to pour out grace and forgiveness to today? Why not thank God today for His wonderful gift of salvation through Christ?

tuesday 2 Samuel 11:1-13

Digging Deeper • David's great sins of immorality and murder are recorded in this chapter. How could one who was "a man after God's own heart" and the sweet psalmist of Israel get so far from God? It happened because he was not doing what he was supposed to be doing—leading his men in battle (v. 1). Then he failed to guard his eyes and his heart (v. 2). He even used his power and position to commit adultery (v. 4). Compare 1 Samuel 2:16 and James 1:15. We should all take heed lest we fall like David did (1 Corinthians 10:11-12). Lust is a very dangerous sin from which we all must guard our hearts and eyes.
Have you ever said, "That will never happen to me"? Instead, pray that God will guard our hearts and eyes from sexual sin. What have you been looking at recently that could cause you to fall?

wednesday 2 Samuel 11:14-27

Digging Deeper • David committed adultery and then set out to devise a plan of deceit to cover his sin. He tried to get Uriah and Bathsheba together so that Uriah would think that the child was his, but sin isn't easily covered up. Nothing seemed to be working to cover up the sin, so David went even further in sin by scheming to murder the man who had shown incredible loyalty, integrity, and valor for his king. More and more people were drawn into the conspiracy and were affected. Joab the general and the unknown messenger were dirtied by David's sin. Did you ever stop to consider how sin runs in packs, and how it always affects others? David's seemingly little glance toward sin got costlier by the moment.

What are you trying to cover? What is the Holy Spirit calling you to confess today? Have you come to realize that there are no "little" sins?

thursday 2 Samuel 12:1-14

Digging Deeper • God often sends a person to warn us of our sinful ways. Sometimes God uses a parent, a teacher, a pastor, or even a friend. God sent David's friend, the prophet Nathan, to warn him of his evil way. Not only did Nathan identify David's sin, but he also told him of its terrible consequences. What David had done in secret had been seen by God, and it would be revealed openly to all. David is forgiven in verse 13, but the consequences of his sin would remain. God still does not overlook sin, so "be not deceived; God is not mocked: for whatsoever a man soweth, that shall he also reap" (Galatians 6:7).

Why not take stock of all the little sins in your life today? What are you doing that you would be ashamed of if God would reveal them to everyone? Pray for a pure heart and mind and life today.

friday 2 Samuel 12:15-31

Digging Deeper • Is there real forgiveness and restoration to the believer who sins grievously against a Holy God? Can God use us again even after we fail Him, humiliate our loved ones, and bring reproach to ourselves? The answer, of course, is YES! David writes four psalms to show his repentance to God. Read them in this order: Psalm 38, 6, 52, and 32. These psalms express the repentance and understanding David had. God gave David a new son named Solomon. God named this son Jedidiah, which means "beloved of the Lord." Nathan was the one who announced God's name for the child, sealing God's forgiveness to David.

Are you ready to be forgiven by the God of the second chance? Why not take time right now to thank the Lord for His forgiveness and restoration?

saturday 2 Samuel 23:1-7

Digging Deeper • If you want to know the rest of the story, you can read about it in chapters 13-24, as they cover the last 20 years of David's life. Finally, in today's passage, we see David's last words as he fully affirms his faith in a faithful God who always keeps His promises and never changes. Many of the Old Testament Scriptures are written to admonish us by giving us examples of how to live and how not to live. David's story gives us the brutal facts, revealing the thrill of victory and the agony of defeat. Behind all this, we see the heart of a loving God that is always willing and able to forgive and pour out grace and mercy on His children.

What will you say in your last words? Will you be deeply in love with your Savior? Will you be convinced, as David was, of God's unquestionable sovereignty?

Week 11

Do you need wisdom? Have you ever been tempted and not known how to keep from failing? Have you ever just not fit in? Do you think others are not good enough for you? Have you ever found a contradiction in Scripture? Have you ever said something you wish you could take back? If so, this week is for you!

prayer focus for this week

the **Question**   **What is the writer saying?**

the **Answer**   **How can I apply this to my life?**

sunday   James 1:1-8

Digging Deeper • As you walk into math class, you see a strange sight. All of your friends are actually studying. "Dude, did you watch the game last night?" you ask. As your best friend totally ignores you, a sickening feeling comes to your stomach. That's right! The big test is today, and you are not prepared. As James writes to Jewish Christians scattered all over the world, he reminds us that the tests and trials that we face in life should not make us queasy, but bring about joy. Joy … because tests bring patience, and patience brings completeness or maturity. However, if we do lack wisdom, we should ask God to give us the wisdom we need, believing that He will provide.

What kinds of tests are you facing today? How can you be joyful in those trials? In what area do you need God's wisdom today?

monday James 1:9-18

Digging Deeper • Have you ever had an opinion about someone, but no solid basis for it? Maybe you have decided that the new, quiet girl is a snob because she hasn't talked to you yet. Perhaps you think the star football player is mentally subpar because he is… well, a football player. Many people have pre-judged God this way. "Since God is all-powerful, He could have stopped that temptation from coming into my life." James reminds us that God does not try to get us to sin. He may test us with difficulties in our lives, but He *never* tempts us to sin. Our own sinful lusts and desires are the source of temptation. God is the giver of good and perfect gifts (v. 17), not temptation (v. 13). God promises a crown for everyone who endures temptation without falling.
How will you yield your desires to Christ this week when you are tempted?

tuesday James 1:19-27

Digging Deeper • Beep! Beep! Beep! The alarm goes off for the fifth time as you finally crawl out of bed. You stumble to the bathroom, picking sleepy dirt out of your eyes. You take one look in the mirror, grab your back pack, and head off to school. Right? Of course not—that would be social suicide. James reminds us that the Word of God is like a mirror for our souls. It shows us where we need work. If we do not act upon what the Bible reveals about our lives, it is like getting out of bed and going straight to school. James reminds us to listen to and linger in the Word (v. 19, 25), lose our wicked ways (v. 21), lasso our own words (v. 26), labor among the widows (v. 27), and leave the way of the world (v. 27).
What does the Bible show you concerning your soul? What changes will you make today as a result of looking into God's Word?

wednesday   James 2:1-9

Digging Deeper • In every high school cafeteria, you will find a reoccurring phenomenon. Each table has a label. The jocks sit in one area, the nerds in another, the mean girls somewhere close to the jocks, and the losers in the back corner. How dare a computer geek think he has the right to sit with the cheerleaders! In James' day, this wasn't taking place in a cafeteria, but in the church. He clearly reminds us not to play favorites ("have respect of persons"). He plainly says that loving your neighbor is good (v. 8), but having respect of persons is sin (v. 9). You are not better than anyone else, regardless of your social status or wealth. Live like a Christian, but do it without playing favorites (v. 1).

How can you show the love of Christ to someone outside of your normal group of friends? Today, try loving your neighbor as yourself.

thursday   James 2:10-18

Digging Deeper • Have you ever met someone who was prone to making up stories? You know — the guy who swears that he talked with LeBron James, the NBA player, last night at Wal-Mart. Maybe it is the girl who got a picture with that famous movie star. It's easy to smirk in unbelief until the guy pulls out LeBron's autograph, or the girl whips out the picture. The Apostle James sports the same smirk of unbelief toward people who say they are Christians but do not live like it. Just like that claim of seeing LeBron James is suspect without the autograph, so are our claims of faith without works. If you claim to have saving faith, prove your faith with your actions. Works will not produce faith, but real faith will work.

How can you show your faith this week by your good works? What Christian Service can you participate in this week?

76

friday James 2:19-26

Digging Deeper • Did you read verse 21? Did it not just say that Abraham was justified by works? Wait a minute! The Bible also says, "For by grace are ye saved through faith... not of works" (Ephesians 2:8-9). What is going on here? Is the Bible contradicting itself? *No way!* Here is the truth: As James is writing about Abraham, he discusses two different time periods of his life. In Genesis 15, Abraham was considered "righteous" by believing God. In Genesis 22, he *proved* his faith by his works. Faith and works go together. If you are truly saved, if you truly have faith, you will prove your faith with your actions. Others cannot tell you are a Christian unless you do something to prove it.

What can you do today? How will you show the world that you have faith in Jesus Christ?

saturday James 3:1-10

Digging Deeper • There is power in small things. The bit is used to turn a horse (v. 3). The helm is used to steer a gigantic ship (v. 4). The spark can ignite a fire that could destroy the largest forest (v. 5). And then there is the tongue... just a small member of your body, but with such potential for destruction (vv. 5-6). The same tongue that praises the Lord often curses man. It is almost as if you can see the Apostle James shaking his head as he writes, "My brethren, these things ought not so to be" (v. 10). James reminds us that if we can just get control of our tongues, we are very mature and capable of controlling the rest of our bodies (v. 2).

How will you control your tongue today? What can you do to stop yourself from using your tongue as a destructive force? Will you commit to pray before you speak?

Did you ever want someone to tell you exactly what to do? If you could just get specific instructions, your life would be a lot easier. Well, this is your week. James gives specific instructions on how to use your time and money, how to be patient, how to be wise, and how to pray. It's simple—just read and apply.

prayer focus for this week

the Question — **What is the writer saying?**

the Answer — **How can I apply this to my life?**

sunday   James 3:11-18

Digging Deeper • Who is the wisest person in your class? Just how wise is your teacher? The world likes to pour out applause on those who are academically intelligent. However, the Bible sees wisdom differently. The Apostle James says that a wise man should perform good works in meekness (v. 13). He also defines heavenly wisdom as "pure, then peaceable, gentle, and easy to be intreated, full of mercy and good fruits, without partiality, and without hypocrisy" (v. 17). In contrast, the wisdom of the world produces "bitter envying and strife," a puffed up attitude, and deceitfulness (v. 14). So, which do you have? We were told in chapter 1 to ask for wisdom if we need it. What type of wisdom do you want?

How can you obtain the wisdom of God? How will you make God's wisdom a priority in your life today?

monday James 4:1-5

Digging Deeper • Do you believe in Santa Claus? Maybe when you were a child and wanted something. But all too often that is how we treat God. "Hey, God, could you give me a… ?" Maybe you take the more spiritual approach, "Our Great and Heavenly Father, wilt Thou please grant me a… ?" Sounds funny, right? In James 4, the people were not getting their prayers answered. James told them that they were asking God for their desires with a selfish motive (v. 3). The people were fighting among themselves, and James reminded them that disunity comes as a result of their own lusts. Because of their selfish *give-me* and *me-first* attitudes and their friendships with the world, they had problems with each other.

How will your prayer life change today as a result of seeing this negative example? Try praying today without asking God for anything.

tuesday James 4:6-10

Digging Deeper • Sometimes Scripture is very easy to apply to everyday living. In today's passage, James is specific and practical: 1. Be humble because God "resisteth (opposes) the proud, but giveth grace to the humble." 2. Be submissive to God and resist the devil, and Satan will have to run. 3. Draw close to God and, in turn, He will draw close to you. 4. Clean up spiritually and be sad about the sin you have allowed to creep into your life. 5. Humble yourself in God's eyes, and He will lift you up.

What can you do today to practice humility? How can you be submissive to God today? In what area will you resist the devil? What action can you take that will draw you closer to God? Will you turn from the sin in your life? What steps will you take today to remove that sin?

Wednesday   James 4:11-17

Digging Deeper • What do you have planned for tomorrow? For next month? What about a year from now? If you are like most of us, you just take for granted that the plans you make will happen. However, the Apostle James warns of boasting about the future. He reminds us that life is short, and God has ultimate control over what we will do. Since life is like a vapor (mist) (v. 14), James reminds us to speak lovingly toward our brothers in Christ and remember that God is the only judge (vv. 11-12). In verse 17, James reminds us that if we know that we should do something good and fail to do it, we are sinning. Whether it is driving the speed limit or cleaning our rooms, we should simply do what we know is right.

Will you surrender your future to God? In what area do you need to decide to simply do right? Toward whom will you begin to speak lovingly?

thursday   James 5:1-6

Digging Deeper • Some students have bought into the "get rich or die tryin'" mentality that the world promotes. You may tell yourself, "This passage is talking to rich people, and I'm not rich." But James reminds all of us that hoarding money will do us no good. He gets specific by condemning the action of accumulating money at the expense of others (v. 4). He rebukes the mentality of living in pleasure on earth by condemning and killing the just (vv. 5-6). Yes, it is easy to condemn the rich for these actions, but you do not have to be rich to sin in this way. The sin of getting money at the expense of others is not limited to the wealthy. You can be poor and have an improper love for money. Your focus must not be about money.

How can you avoid an unbiblical focus on money? What will you do today to keep your focus on Christ?

friday James 5:7-12

Digging Deeper • "I just can't wait until schools out." "I can't wait until this weekend." "I'm starving! I can't wait until dinner. I gotta eat something now!" Have you ever said something like that? Sure you have. Haven't we all? In today's passage, James focuses on patience. He lets us know that Jesus is coming back and that we should patiently wait for His return. By reminding us of the suffering of the prophets and the endurance of Job, he encourages us to live patiently. Finally, James commands us not to resort to taking oaths as proof of our honesty, but simply to say what we mean and mean what we say.

How can you be more patient today as you wait for the return of Christ?
How can the example of Job and other heroes of the faith encourage you?

saturday James 5:13-20

Digging Deeper • Prayer is a powerful thing. If we have a physical problem, we should call for the elders of the church to pray. If we have a problem with a brother in Christ, we are to confess our faults and pray for each other. James reminds us that prayer is so powerful that when Elijah prayed for a drought, it did not rain for three and a half years! Prayer can change our lives. However, notice the stipulations on effective prayer. In verse 16, James says, "The effectual fervent prayer of a righteous man availeth much." Our prayers must be fervent, enthusiastic, avid, ardent, and impassioned. Secondly, for our prayers to have any effect, we must be righteous.

Will you commit to following God's pattern for problem-solving through prayer?
What sin do you need to forsake in order for your prayers to be effective? Will you forsake it today?

Would you pay attention if the wisest person who ever lived offered to give you advice? Solomon shares his advice for recognizing a wicked person, how wise and foolish people handle their "stuff," and even how to make your parents proud of you. Get ready to gain wisdom and understanding!

prayer focus for this week

 the Question

 the Answer

What is the writer saying?

How can I apply this to my life?

sunday   Proverbs 21:1-12

Q

A

Digging Deeper • What we choose to do shows what is really in our hearts. Think about the idea of a "wicked" person—what would his or her actions look like? Solomon tells us that God weighs the heart by knowing the motives behind our actions (v. 2). Solomon describes the wicked person using the following characteristics: he is violent (v. 7); he refuses to live justly (v. 7); he desires evil (v. 10); he is impossible to please, looking critically at those around him (v. 10); he ends in destruction at the hand of a righteous God (v. 12). Above all, a wicked person may think his or her way of living is acceptable (v. 2), while he or she is actually displeasing God.

Who controls your heart and discerns your motives? Do you have any of the characteristics of the wicked? What is one thing you can do differently today to let God control more of your heart?

monday Proverbs 21:13-22

Digging Deeper • How do you react when you see someone truly in need? Do you look away, hoping someone else will help them? Solomon said that if we don't help the needy, we'll suffer the same fate someday (v. 13) (see also James 2:15-17 and 1 John 3:17). Solomon says the differences between the foolish and the wise are the way they handle their possessions and wealth. The foolish pursue pleasure (v. 17) and squander things of value (v. 20). The wise, on the other hand, give gifts the right way (v. 14), enjoy justice (v. 15), understands the value of saving (v. 20), and seek after righteousness and love to find life, prosperity, and honor (v. 21).

Seek out and help someone in need with your time, knowledge, or money. In what ways are you foolish or wise in the way you handle your possessions?

tuesday Proverbs 21:23-31

Digging Deeper • After reading today's passage, which of these would you say your tongue is: controlled, proud, lazy, wicked, or lying? It's not a trick question. Of course, everyone wants to say controlled, but what does your actual speech reveal? What would people around you say? Is your speech proud (v. 24), greedy (v. 26), or full of lies (false witness v. 28)? Or is it guarded (v. 23), giving (v. 26), and thoughtful (v. 29)? Solomon tells us throughout the book of Proverbs that the tongue acts as an indicator of our spiritual state and character. If we guard and control our tongue, it will keep us from all kinds of trouble in life.

What does your everyday speech reveal about your character? Decide now to pause and think before you speak to everyone you meet today. Find someone who could use a kind word and choose to bless them.

wednesday Proverbs 22:1-16

Digging Deeper • Would you rather be rich or poor? Most of us would probably rather be somewhere in the middle—not having the hardships of the poor or the responsibilities of the rich. Solomon addresses our attitude toward the rich and the poor several times in this passage. A good name is better than wealth (v. 1). God made both the rich and the poor (v. 2). Being humble and fearing the Lord brings true riches, honor, and life (v. 4). The borrower becomes the servant to the lender (v. 7). The generous person who shares with the poor will be blessed (v. 9), but those who oppress the poor will come to want things themselves (v. 16).
Knowing that God made you and has a tender heart toward the poor, what can you do to show generosity to someone in need?

thursday Proverbs 22:17-29

Digging Deeper • Would you listen if the smartest, wisest person you knew of offered to tell you the secrets to life and death? This passage opens with two commands from Solomon, the wisest man who ever lived. First, we are to listen to the words of the wise. Second, we are to apply that knowledge to our heart. We will have a pleasant life if we follow these guidelines (v. 18). His words of wisdom include trusting in the Lord (v. 19), caring for the poor and needy (v. 22), not being friends with an angry person (v. 24), not pledging to pay a debt for someone else if they can't pay (v. 26), not moving boundaries (v. 28), and being a good worker (v. 29).
Ask God to show you one wise thing from this passage that you need to work on. Find a way to apply it to your life today.

fr̄idəy Proverbs 23:1-14

Digging Deeper • Do you know why Solomon is telling us to watch what we eat and how we work? It's a lot more than just being careful to use our best manners when we're with "high society" or working hard to earn a living—it shows whether we have true understanding. To gain understanding and wisdom is an important theme throughout the book of Proverbs (1:1-6). Solomon shares some cautions about our priorities on wealth and work. There is nothing wrong with having wealth; what's important is whether or not we are controlled by it. We need to assess our priorities and not set our sights on something that is fleeting (v. 5) but rather on "understanding"—that which is stable, dependable, and leads to wisdom.
Think about your priorities about wealth and work. Are you working hard to get rich? What are you doing to pursue understanding?

saturdəy Proverbs 23:15-25

Digging Deeper • What makes most parents the happiest? Is it having children who are popular or who are "stars" on the field or in the classroom? Nope! It is having children who make good outward choices, reflecting an inner wisdom (vv. 15-16; 24-25). People can tell children have wisdom in their hearts by the way they speak. What does that look like? First, they will not be envious of others (v. 17). Second, they choose to make good friends—here, that does not include those given to excesses of wine or food, which brings laziness and poverty (v. 21). A wise child/person seeks out truth, wisdom, discipline, and understanding (v. 23).
Are you envious of others, or is the focus of your life finding true inner wisdom? How does your choice of friends help you in this pursuit? How can you practically find truth, wisdom, discipline, or understanding today?

Week 14.

Are you ready for another exciting week to gain wisdom and understanding? This week Solomon gives advice about sex, alcohol, and how to deal with enemies. If that's not enough, we'll also learn about what our attitudes, words, and work have to say about us. Are you up to the challenge?

prayer focus for this week

theQuestion
theAnswer

What is the writer saying?

How can I apply this to my life?

sunday Proverbs 23:26-35

Q

A

Digging Deeper • What do you do when all the voices around you says it is okay to have sex outside of marriage and to drink all the alcohol you want? The Bible tells us they are both wrong. Solomon told his son (and us) in this passage to observe him and follow the example he set specifically in these two areas. Proverbs is full of passages warning men to stay away from wicked women (chapters 6-7). Any man who falls for these schemes will face peril and destruction (vv. 27-28). Second, Solomon warns his son (and us) to stay away from strong drink because it dulls the senses, causes disgraceful speech, and begins the downward spiral of domination (vv. 31-35). Is that what you want for your future?

Looking at these warnings, what do you think your approach to sex and alcohol should be, compared to what you may be hearing from the world?

monday Proverbs 24:1-12

Digging Deeper • What do you look for when forming a new friendship or relationship? Can you tell early on what a person is truly like from the way he speaks? Solomon warns us not to make friends with or be envious of evil men. Their speech reveals a heart attitude bent toward violence and causing trouble (vv. 1-2, 8). Solomon tells us (again) to seek out wisdom. When you are making wise choices and have friends around you who are also trying to make wise choices, you will be strong (v. 5), successful and safe (v. 6), and lifted above foolish people (v. 7). What do the choices you make in your friendships reveal about you?

What does the speech of your friends reveal? What does *your* speech reveal? How does your speech or choice of friends need to change in order to follow what you've learned from this passage?

tuesday Proverbs 24:13-22

Digging Deeper • How can you tell the difference between a righteous person and a wicked person? Does it help to watch how a person interacts with others? What do you watch for? Solomon uses nine tips in this section to teach us how to live wisely as we watch those around us. A correct attitude toward the wicked would be to not be happy when they fall (v. 17) nor worry about or be envious of them (v. 19). We need to have a wise, long-term perspective, understanding both the hope of the righteous (v. 14) and the certain calamity of the wicked at the hand of a righteous God (vv. 16, 20, 22).

Are you making wise and righteous choices? Is there someone around you who is not? How can you live today with the hope of the righteous rather than envying the short-term success of those not living in a godly way?

wednesday   Proverbs 24:23-34

Digging Deeper • Two themes come through in this passage: what our words say about us, and what our work says about us. Solomon condemns words that show partiality. He gives us examples of both the one who is partial and the one who is just, plus the consequences of each (vv. 23-25). The word lazy (sluggard) is used fifteen times in the Old Testament; fourteen are in Proverbs. In verses 30-34 Solomon talks about our work ethic and the result of being lazy, which is poverty. When it comes to work, we should do it right the first time for we never get a second chance to make a good first impression. Our approach to work should be: Do it. Do it right. Do it right now. Procrastination only leads to laziness.
What do your words and work ethic say about you? What can you change today to make yourself a more diligent worker?

thursday   Proverbs 25:1-10

Digging Deeper • If you were invited to the Governor's mansion, Capitol Hill, or the White House, how would you act and what would you say? It would be pretty intimidating for most people. You would wear your best clothes and use your best manners, of course. Solomon shares some wisdom here on how to handle any situation with those in authority. Be humble! It would be better to be humble than humiliated in front of those who are in authority (vv. 6-7). Humility also applies to our everyday actions and in our attitude to those around us (v. 8).
Are you a humble person before an Almighty God and King? How about those in authority? What about with your family and peers? It never hurts to be humble!

friday · Proverbs 25:11-20

Digging Deeper • When was the last time someone said something to you that was exactly what you needed to hear at that moment? What about when something unnecessary or cruel was said? Both situations have probably happened to you, and unfortunately, by you. Solomon illustrates the power and influence words can have—to be used either positively or negatively. Right words spoken at the right time are a thing of beauty (v. 12). The outcome of a confrontation between two wise people is beautiful, while that same confrontation when one of them is a fool is not so pretty (vv. 18-19).

Are your words a thing of beauty? In what specific ways have you seen wisdom or foolishness reflected in your words? Look for an opportunity to bless someone with your words.

saturday · Proverbs 25:21-28

Digging Deeper • There is a lot of wisdom in these verses about how to treat your enemies, caution to take with a contentious wife, the danger of seeking your own glory, and the result of having no self-control. Listen to what the Lord has for you. We'll look at Solomon's wisdom on how to respond to an enemy. Where we would naturally respond with revenge, he commands us to provide for our enemies' needs. The Mosaic Law gives the same guideline (Leviticus 19:17-18). Jesus also speaks of this in His Sermon on the Mount (Matthew 5:43-48). Paul even quotes this passage when instructing the Roman believers (Romans 12:14, 17-21). We are to trust God with any situation. He is all-knowing and powerful, and He has a plan. We need to learn to trust His justice, mercy, and love.

Who is someone you need to show kindness or love to today?

As you look into the Scripture this week, Peter will give some basic instructions for living the Christian life. He will remind you of your future and what God did for you. He will give you some practical advice for living in a godly way. When this week is finished, you should be excited about being on God's team. Read on!

prayer focus for this week

the Question
the Answer

What is the writer saying?

How can I apply this to my life?

sunday 1 Peter 1:1-8

Q

A

Digging Deeper • As you walk into the room, you see the perfect place to sit. How in the world did everyone else miss it? As you get closer, you see the sign: *Reserved*. Reserved —what a frustrating word that can be—unless, of course, it is reserved for you. As Peter begins his letter to believers scattered throughout the region, he reminds them that because they are saved, they have a place set aside for them in Heaven. What a joy to know that all Christians are kept by the power of God (v. 5)! Despite what trials (vv. 6-7) the world may send our way, and despite the fact that we have never seen Jesus (v. 8), we can be joyful because our future is secure. We have a place reserved for us.

Stop right now and thank God that He makes your future secure. Who do you know that may need you to explain the way to a secure future to them?

monday 1 Peter 1:9-16

Digging Deeper • So, you are saved! You asked Jesus to be your Savior, and you are not going to Hell. And that's it! Sadly, that *is* it for a lot of immature Christians. "Don't ask me to live like a Christian," they say with their lifestyle. "That ain't cool." The Apostle Peter, however, makes some pretty bold statements. He says, "Not fashioning (conforming) yourselves according to your former lusts (evil desires)." In other words, the way you handle yourself should not be like the world. In contrast, you should live holy—totally separate from sin and evil. The way you dress should be holy. The way you talk should be holy. The way you look should be holy. The things you listen to or look at should be holy. "Be ye holy in all manner of conversation (lifestyle)…be ye holy, for I am holy" (vv. 15-16).
What part of your lifestyle looks like the world? What needs to change?

tuesday 1 Peter 1:17-25

Digging Deeper • What is the most expensive gift you have ever received? How did you respond when you got it? It feels great to get a gift of such value. The Apostle Peter reminds us of a priceless gift that was given for us. God had a plan, even before the world began (v. 20), for Jesus to die for us. It was a gift more expensive than gold or silver (v. 18). God thought about us! Furthermore, if we have accepted His great gift of love, we should love the brethren (v. 22). As if the gift was not enough, Peter reminds us that the gift is secure.
When is the last time you thanked God for thinking about you in such a profound way? With whom will you share your gift?

wednesday 1 Peter 2:1-10

Digging Deeper • Can you remember what it was like when you first joined a sports team, or when you got that new job? You may not have known exactly how to act or what to do. Hopefully at some point, a coach, boss, teammate, or co-worker made you feel like you were really part of the team. Peter reminds us of the team we have joined—that we are part of the body of Christ (v. 5) and that Jesus is the chief cornerstone (v. 6). We have been chosen and called out of darkness (v. 9), and we have obtained God's mercy (v. 10). He also reminds us that our "cornerstone" is offensive to some (vv. 7-8). Being a Christian is so much more than the individual Christian, because we are part of something greater than ourselves.

How can you be more of a "team player" this week? How can you show the praises of the Lord Jesus Christ?

thursday 1 Peter 2:11-17

Digging Deeper • "I thought you were a Christian." Those are sad words to have to hear. The Apostle Peter strongly encourages each Christian to live in the world but separate from it. The world loves to speak out against God's people, and when a Christian openly sins, it gives the unsaved world ammunition to take a shot at the name of Christ. Peter urges us to be submissive to the rules of men and to place ourselves openly under the appropriate authorities. By doing so, we can shut the mouths of any would-be mud-slingers. Remember, this world is not our permanent home. We are but "strangers and pilgrims" (v. 11).

What steps can you take to protect your name, the name of your church, and the precious name of Jesus from those who would defame them?

friday · 1 Peter 2:18-25

Digging Deeper • Occasionally in sports, a player will take a cheap shot at another player. He might make a late hit after the whistle blows. He might push or tackle away from the play, or he might slide into second base with his spikes high. But do you know who usually gets into trouble? Not the cheap shot guy but the guy who retaliates. Peter reminds us of how we are to act when we get the short end of the stick. He tells us that God is pleased when we receive persecution patiently. Our example is Jesus Christ Himself. He deserved none of what He endured on the cross. Yet as He hung there, His only words about those who were killing Him were words of forgiveness. He is our example—follow His steps.

In what area of life are you experiencing suffering? How can you be like Christ in that area? Will you follow the suffering steps of Jesus?

saturday · 1 Peter 3:1-7

Digging Deeper • So, you're not a wife and you're not a husband, therefore, this passage doesn't apply to you, right? Wrong! Oh, you may not be married right now, but one day you might be, and these lessons are so much easier to learn now than they will be later. Ladies, decide right now that when you are married you will live in subjection to your husband. Begin adorning yourself, not with a bunch of clothes that draw attention to your body, but by putting on a meek and quiet spirit. Commit to keeping yourself pure for your future husband. Guys, determine right now that forsaking all others, you will love the girl you will one day marry. Love her so much that, even now, you will keep yourself pure for only her.

What can you do right now that will improve your future marriage? How can you prepare yourself for your future spouse?

The Christian life is not all fun and games. Unfortunately, the Christian life can be difficult and filled with suffering. This week, Peter will give you some practical advice on how to deal with undeserved suffering. He will discuss the hard work that it takes to live godly. Hang on for some help with the difficult times in life.

prayer focus for this week

the Question — What is the writer saying?

the Answer — How can I apply this to my life?

sunday 1 Peter 3:8-12

Q

A

Digging Deeper • Have you ever wondered what it would take to have a good life? Maybe if you had brand-name clothes, a fancy foreign car, stacks of cash, and the face of a movie star, you would have a good life. If you watch television or go to the movies, those things seem to be the secret. Well, here is the *real* secret. If you want to "love life and see good days" (v. 10), you must speak no evil (v. 10), see no evil (v. 11), and seek peace (v. 11). Since God is watching the righteous and listening to their prayers, we should live in unity with love and courtesy. When someone does us wrong, we should not return the wrongdoing, but give him the mercy of a blessing. What is your life like? Are you trying to find the *good life*?
From what evil do you need to run? What steps do you need to take to be more unified with your fellow Christians?

monday 1 Peter 3:13-22

Digging Deeper • Today's topic: More suffering. "Oh, great," you say, "that's really encouraging." Actually, it can be encouraging. We know that we are going to suffer, but "who is he that will harm you [us], if ye [we] be followers of that which is good?" Peter reminds us that, in the midst of the suffering, we should have already decided that God will be our priority and that we will use suffering as an opportunity to share our faith. Jesus, Who did not deserve to die, suffered and died for us. He is our example. If the ungodly world tries to accuse us of evil, our lifestyle should be so holy that no one would ever believe the lie (v. 16).

Does your lifestyle cause others to ask about Jesus? If the world made accusations against your Christian character, would others believe them? What can you do this week to strengthen your character?

tuesday 1 Peter 4:1-6

Digging Deeper • If someone in your school hosted a party involving an illegal activity, would you get invited? The question is not "Would you go?" but "Would you get invited?" Do you have a reputation that excludes you from such invitations? Do you live in such a way that others know not to even give you an invitation because you would never entertain the thought of attending? Peter, speaking of fellow believers, reports that the world thinks it is strange that these believers do not act the way they used to (vv. 3-4). As a result, they received undeserved scorn. Remember, we will ultimately be judged by Jesus Christ. Live today in such a way as to please Him, not the "in crowd."

Do you "fit in" with ungodly people? How have you changed since accepting Christ as your Savior? How will you improve your reputation as a believer?

wednesday 1 Peter 4:7-11

Digging Deeper • How much do you love others? Peter very clearly says, "above all things have fervent charity [love] among yourselves" (v. 8). Since we are to have love "above all," how should we go about loving others? Well, verse 9 tells us to be hospitable and not hold grudges. Verse 10 tells us to use the gift, talent, or ability that we have to minister to others. So, naturally, we can show our love to others in these three ways: be hospitable, do not hold grudges, and minister with our abilities. If you do not have a specific opportunity to use your spiritual gift, contact your pastor or youth pastor for some suggestions. As we love in these ways, God is glorified (v. 11).

To whom can you be hospitable this week? How will you do it? What gifts have you been given? How will you use them this week?

thursday 1 Peter 4:12-19

Digging Deeper • Have you ever watched a news report that showed someone being arrested? Many times the suspect will hide his face in shame. His unlawful actions are the cause for coming problems. His future suffering is well-deserved. But what about those who suffer because they are Christians? Peter encourages them to hold their heads up high because their suffering in Christ shows that the Spirit of God is upon them (v. 14). However, Peter warns us to live righteously so we do not receive deserved suffering. He also reminds us that when God judges, He starts with His own children (v. 17). Live in such a way that He will be glorified.

How can you give God glory through your suffering? If God were to judge you today, what would be the outcome? What can you work on this week that would help you be prepared for coming judgment?

friday 1 Peter 5:1-7

Digging Deeper • How do you feel when someone tells you to do something that they refuse to do themselves? It is kind of frustrating, isn't it? Peter gave the elders of the church a few basic instructions. He told them to take charge of the children of God (v. 2). They were not supposed to be *dictators*, but rather examples of how to live. We are to follow the example of the elders and be humble. In doing so, God will exalt us when the time is right (v. 6). How much easier it is to be humble when our elders are humble! Even Peter shows his willingness to follow his own teaching. In verse 1, while speaking of himself, he says, "who am also an elder." Peter lived what he preached. Because he is a great example, we can find it easier to obey.

Do you practice what you preach? What kind of example are you to those who are younger? How can you improve this week?

saturday 1 Peter 5:8-14

Digging Deeper • Have you ever seen someone pretend to be a basketball superstar? As he shoots the ball, he can be heard saying, "Three, two, one—it's over! We win!" You don't often see someone in the push-up position, acting like a hero. The truth is that months of training, a dedication to the game, and hard work are the real reasons for the glory. The last-second shot can happen because the work has already taken place. The athlete must suffer before he will receive glory. Peter reminds us that we are called to glory (v. 10), but we must first endure suffering. The suffering will mature, establish, strengthen, and settle us (v. 10). When that happens, God can be glorified in our lives.

What is your attitude toward suffering? Begin today to grow and bring glory to God.

Week 17

This is the perfect time to read about Jesus coming into the world. It is an amazing story! The people, and lessons they learn, can be surprising. Maybe we would have written the story differently, but God made it perfect. There's much to learn in this first week of Luke. Don't miss it!

prayer focus for this week

the Question — What is the writer saying?
the Answer — How can I apply this to my life?

sunday   Luke 1:1-12

Digging Deeper • Luke tells Theophilus he's going to write about Christ's life. Interestingly enough, Luke starts off talking about ordinary people (Zechariah and Elisabeth) before Jesus was even born. Have you ever felt plain, ordinary, or as if God would never use you for big things? That's great—you're just the kind of person God can use! It was an ordinary day for an ordinary priest. Zechariah and Elisabeth probably had no idea of God's great plans for them, but verse 6 describes why God would use them. Often, we're only moments away from God's special tasks for us when we decide to get discouraged. Just keep being faithful!

What sin is keeping you from being used by God? Are you currently being faithful in all your responsibilities?

monday Luke 1:13-25

Digging Deeper • Verse 13 tells us that Zechariah had been praying for a child. How amazing it would have been to have an angel tell you face to face that your prayer had been answered. This wasn't just any child though—verses 14-17 describe what an amazing man of God he would become. Zechariah was surprised, but he had been praying for this very thing; perhaps he did not trust that God would really answer his prayer this way. Even though Zechariah wasn't perfect through all this, the Lord was still going to use him.

When you pray, do you expect God to answer your request? When you finish praying about difficult times, do you still worry? How can you trust God more with the uncertainties you are facing this week?

tuesday Luke 1:26-38

Digging Deeper • Today we are introduced to Mary, the mother of Jesus. Although she was "highly favored" (v. 28) by the Lord, she was just an ordinary young girl whom God chose to give birth to His Son—not someone to be worshipped in herself. She was highly favored because she was godly, as you can tell in her response (vv. 34, 38). Like Zechariah, Mary questioned, "How this could be?", but she didn't doubt. She simply asked how it was going to happen since she was a virgin. Verses 35-38 are an excellent example of God explaining how life was going to be for Mary, followed by a correct response from her. I'm sure she didn't understand everything, but she *undoubtedly* showed faith.

Have you ever been confused about God's plan for you? Are you responding like Mary? Do you need to respond in faith to a situation now?

wednesday Luke 1:39-56

Digging Deeper • If we were Mary, we might have wanted to run and tell one of our relatives our exciting news also! Whether or not Mary knew Elisabeth was also with child is uncertain, but what a wonderful surprise. Elisabeth was someone who understood what Mary was experiencing. God met Mary's need of friendship. Verses 46-55 are a beautiful song of Mary. She was learning the Lord's design for her, but it didn't happen immediately. Look at how long she was with Elisabeth (v. 56). In three months you can get to know someone really well.

Are you ever impatient with God because you don't understand His design? Are you praising Him anyway?

thursday Luke 1:57-66

Digging Deeper • Elisabeth finally had her child. In modern times, we pick out names before a child is born, but Jewish culture waited until the eighth day. It was very popular for firstborn sons to be named after their father, but not this time. God had already told Zechariah to name his son "John" (Luke 1:13), and Zechariah had learned his lesson (to trust God). He asked no questions and threw tradition aside. He did what God had told him to, and we see the results in verse 64. Wow! That started people talking. We now know Zechariah as the man who obeyed God, not one who doubted Him. What an impact his obedience had on people all over the hill country of Judea. The Lord is just waiting to use you also!

Have you ever doubted God? Did you ever finally trust Him? Is there any area right now where you need to submit to God and trust Him?

friday Luke 1:67-80

Digging Deeper • Zechariah was silent the whole time he was waiting for John to be born. Imagine actually prophesying about the future so quickly! The first half of Zechariah's prophesy is referring to Christ. The "horn of salvation" refers to a powerful person who will bring salvation. Jesus Christ will be the fulfillment of the covenant God made with Abraham. In verse 76, Zechariah refers to John, calling him the person that prepares the way for Jesus Christ, just like the angel mentioned earlier in the chapter. Consider how long John the Baptist had to prepare for that ministry. All those years in the desert helped him learn how to be just the right person God wanted him to be. God is preparing you now for your future as well.
What can you learn now that God can use in the future? Are you being patient as you wait for God to prepare you?

saturday Luke 2:1-14

Digging Deeper • Imagine your Christmas starting off with a 70-mile hike from Nazareth to Bethlehem while you were pregnant! There's no room at the hotel, and you end up staying in a stable that was probably full of animals to give birth to God's Son. The neat thing about this passage is you don't hear any complaining from Joseph or Mary. There was no little crib or fancy baby blanket—just a feeding trough and some strips of cloth. Imagine heavenly royalty being born in such a place. What surveyor's chain could ever measure from Heaven's majesty to that lowly manger? God's love and mercy goes far beyond our comprehension.
Are you thankful for what the Lord has given you this day? When was the last time you were not thankful? What can you do to have a more thankful attitude?

Week 18

This week, we close the chapter on John the Baptist, but more importantly, we see Jesus grow from a baby to an adult. Have you ever wondered what Jesus was like as a teenager? Have you ever wondered how He responded to His parents? You won't want to miss a day!

prayer focus for this week

the Question — What is the writer saying?

the Answer — How can I apply this to my life?

sunday   Luke 2:15-24

Digging Deeper • Hopefully, this is the time of year that we are more aware and conscious of Christ than ever. In fact, I wonder if we are ever as excited about Christ as these shepherds were. We know they were excited because of the action they took, as seen in verses 15-17: "Let us go *now*," "came with *haste*," "they made *widely* known." People responded by marveling and pondering those things. That's what happens when we share Christ! A genuinely excited Christian will readily take action and speak of the Savior with great joy, especially during appropriate seasonal events.

Are you afraid to talk about Christ with others? What is the name of one person you will tell about Christ this week?

monday Luke 2:25-38

Digging Deeper • We are introduced to two interesting individuals, Simeon and Anna. People didn't know how God was going to help Israel, but these two did. Imagine being Simeon, knowing you would see the Messiah before you died, and waiting all that time. Jesus is only eight days old and already He is being revealed as the Savior! Simeon said Jesus would cause the falling and rising of many in Israel. That's true of people today as well. People either believe He is their Savior (making them rise), or they stumble all their lives, never knowing Christ personally (fall). When people are introduced to Jesus, what is inside their heart is truly revealed. He is either our Savior or He isn't.

Who do you know that is stumbling over Christ? When people speak of Jesus, are you ashamed to speak freely of His awesome salvation?

tuesday Luke 2:39-52

Digging Deeper • We learn so much about Christ in today's passage. He was fully God, and He knew the Father wanted Him in the temple courts, asking questions and answering the other teachers. He was perfectly tuned in to the Father's will. That's why He asked His mother, "Didn't you know ...?" She was only human as we are and still had much to learn about the Father's will. Jesus was also fully man. He grew, just like us. As a human child, He grew physically, socially, and mentally. He learned how to think and understand just as we did as twelve-year-olds. If Jesus needed to grow in His ability to think and understand, how much more do we? We certainly aren't God as Jesus was. We need to follow His example.

Does it bother you when your parents try to teach you something? Do you really desire to learn and grow, or do you act like you know it all?

wednesday Luke 3:1-14

Digging Deeper • Eighteen years have gone by since we saw John in chapter one. Verses 4-6 are quoted from Isaiah 40, with John fulfilling those prophecies. The people who came to see John had a major problem. They were very religious and looked good on the outside, but inside, their hearts were still far from God. They were to produce fruit, which meant they were supposed to *prove* they had a heart for God; but the fruit was missing. John mentions that trees that don't bear fruit get cut down and thrown into the fire. It's the same with people. For those that don't know Christ, Hell certainly awaits. Good fruit doesn't keep salvation; it is just proof of it. Do you have proof?

What's more important, your inside heart for God or your outward show? Do you put on a spiritual show for people, or is there real fruit in your life?

thursday Luke 3:15-22

Digging Deeper • Luke finishes writing about John and begins his account of Jesus. People mistook John the Baptist for Christ, but John readily let them know that the Messiah would begin His earthly ministry soon. John wanted no glory or recognition, but instead pointed people to Christ. He was very humble about not even being worthy to untie Jesus' sandals. John 3:28-30 shows more of John's humble attitude. John ended up being the one who baptized Jesus (Mark 1:9). The Lord has many amazing things for us to do for Him. We ought to be as humble as John was—never puffed up!

Who gets the credit when we do things for the Lord? Do you, or do you just thank God for it? Are you being humble like John was?

friday Luke 3:23-38

Digging Deeper • Is this a hard one today? Is this just a bunch of names, or can we really learn something here? You bet we can! This traces Jesus' family (Mary's side) from Him all the way back to Adam—the very first human from Genesis! Compare these verses to these names: verse 31 (1 Samuel 16:1, 13); verse 34 (Genesis 12:1-3); verse 36 (Genesis 6:9); and verse 37 (Genesis 5:21-24). What a heritage! Who in your family history were men and women of God? Maybe you could be one of the first to start a godly heritage. What will your children and grandchildren say about you 60 years from now?
What kind of legacy are you going to leave? Will your children be able to say that their father or mother was godly, even as teenagers?

saturday Luke 4:1-15

Digging Deeper • Have you ever thought about verses 1 and 2? Do you realize that God, the Holy Spirit, led Jesus into the desert to be tempted? God didn't do the tempting, but He allowed it. Satan, who acted when Jesus was physically weak, also knows the best time to tempt us. We need to be on guard and prepared. If we respond to Satan's tempting correctly, God knows we can only grow stronger from it. The key was how Jesus responded to the temptation. He used the same method each time. When tempted to do something He knew He shouldn't, He answered with Scripture. Are you ready to handle Satan's attack with Scripture? It could be today! *No verses? No victory! Know verses—know victory!*
How does Satan tempt you the most? What verses do you need to memorize today?

This week you will discover new ways to learn truth: Through an authoritative teacher, by some miracles, the calling of the disciples, and a showdown with the Pharisees! Jesus brings out critical lessons in each of these situations you won't want to miss. The news of Jesus is spreading, bringing blessings and challenges.

prayer focus for this week

the Question — What is the writer saying?

the Answer — How can I apply this to my life?

sunday   Luke 4:16-30

Q

A

Digging Deeper • Jesus had already been teaching and doing miracles throughout the land, and eventually He returned to His hometown of Nazareth. The people were amazed that this was the same little boy who grew up right before their eyes—this Jesus, Who was the fulfillment of what was read in the book of Isaiah and the One that frees people from sin and gives sight to blind men. The people expected the One Who would fulfill this prophecy to be a highly respected, strong individual with a perfect social status, not the little boy who grew up in town. God often uses the unexpected to help us grow and change. We always need to be ready to learn.

Is your heart hard like the hearts of these people? Are you ready to learn at all times? Can you think of someone you can learn from that you may not expect?

monday Luke 4:31-44

Digging Deeper • We now see Jesus doing miracles of healing. He healed anything from demon possession to high fevers. Note that Jesus healed everyone that came to Him. Nobody left disappointed! It was because He had both the love and authority to do it, unlike so-called healers of today. But the important part about today's passage is not the healing. The key is verse 43—preaching the good news! The greatest miracles were people hearing the good news and God changing their hearts and minds, not just their bodies. The good news is that God has given you authority to teach and share the good news. Are you ready to be a part of this miracle?

What's the name of one person with whom you can share Christ this week? Would you be willing to ask God to help you do that?

tuesday Luke 5:1-11

Digging Deeper • Today, Jesus is picking His disciples, specifically Peter. Peter was a good fisherman, and he knew nighttime was a good time to fish, but only in shallow water. It made no sense to fish in "deep" water. Most fishermen probably wouldn't take advice from a carpenter's son, but Peter responded like all of us should: "at your word," or "because you said so." How many blessings does the Lord have reserved for us if we would just follow His Word, even when it doesn't make sense? Peter realized he had a great need for the Lord when he didn't even feel worthy to be in His presence.

Where do you want the Lord to bless you? How are you not following God's Word so that He can bless you? How desperate is your need for Christ?

wednesday Luke 5:12-26

Digging Deeper • Two more people are healed, each with similar lessons. The first miracle about the man with leprosy is interesting, because Leviticus 13:45 says that anyone with leprosy should cry out "unclean" so that people would know to stay away. This person didn't do that, though. He knew that Jesus was the only one who could heal him, so he asked for cleansing. The faith of the other man's friends was remarkable. They knew if they could only get close and were willing to ask, the Lord would heal their friend. In fact, they didn't let anything stand in their way of getting to Jesus. Our faith should be no different.

Do you believe the Lord wants to help you in life, if you only ask? What obstacles keep you from praying and asking Him to use His power in your life?

thursday Luke 5:27-39

Digging Deeper • Today is the calling of Jesus' disciple Levi, who was also called Matthew. He was a tax collector, a job where extra money could easily be taken from people. These men were usually pretty rich and not very well-liked (tax collectors were also known simply as "sinners"). Matthew responded to Jesus' call like all of us should. After an invitation with Matthew's friends, Jesus could have responded in a different way. He could have not accepted the offer so that He wouldn't be seen with such a terrible group of people. But He realized that all men need a Savior—especially those caught in sin. That's why Jesus responded like He did. He wasn't part of the world, but He still ministered in it.

Can you think of any lost people you need to share Christ with that frighten you? How can you share Christ with them in some way this week?

friday Luke 6:1-12

Digging Deeper • The Sabbath was a Jewish person's holy day of the week. An important part of the day was that there was no work. Jesus, being God, actually created this Holy day for the Jews in history past. By picking the heads of grain, the Pharisees accused Jesus of harvesting, saying that was "work." Because Jesus healed people, they twisted Jesus' miracles into being "work" also. Jesus shows them their thinking was in error. These Pharisees stretched the rule to mean more than it did. Picking a little grain to eat, or doing good like Jesus' healing, was never wrong! Biblical standards are good, but stretching them out of bounds to say what we want is error. That's what the Pharisees' hearts led them to do.

What is the condition of your heart? Have you ever stretched God's Word to make it say what you want?

saturday Luke 6:13-26

Digging Deeper • This is a key text of Jesus' teaching. It is known as the "beatitudes." The people in verses 24-26 thought that if they were rich, had plenty to eat, were always happy, and had a great reputation, they were spiritual. They assumed God would never allow a sinful person to have all these things. Jesus set the record straight. There were plenty of poor people who were far more spiritual than those who had a lot. In fact, many of the poor people of Jesus' day were more spiritual, because it was the eternal things that were important to them—not the money, food, happiness, or reputation on earth. Sometimes doing what is honoring to God is hard and even unpopular. Would you rather please God or the world?

Are you "blessed," according to verses 20-22? Do you value the things of earth or the things of Heaven?

We are entering the bulk of Jesus' teachings this week. He taught publicly from the Old Testament and used miracles and parables to teach others. Pay attention to the different ways people responded to Jesus' teaching as you do your Quiet Time this week.

prayer focus for this week

the Question
the Answer

What is the writer saying?

How can I apply this to my life?

sunday Luke 6:27-38

Digging Deeper • We may not have serious enemies, but most of us know of someone who doesn't like us. But if we were to bless them and treat them like we would like to be treated, we might see even fewer fit into that category. It's easy to love people who love us, but love like the Father's (v. 36) is much greater than that. It's a good thing, too, because Christ died for us while we were His enemies (Philippians 3:18-20). Because He did die for His enemies, many people are now at peace with Him. Perhaps if we had that kind of love for others, they would respond to Christ and no longer be either His or our enemy.

Who makes you angry quicker than anyone else? What are you going to do this week to show them God's unconditional love?

monday Luke 6:39-49

Digging Deeper • Today's verses build to the crucial question of, "Do we truly love God enough to obey Him?" If we do, four things will be true:

1) You won't follow false teachers. Those are people that perhaps sound biblical but are actually blind.

2) You won't live a life of hypocrisy where it is easier to make hasty judgments about friends and people without considering your own life first.

3) Because of the condition of your heart, there will be good fruit (words and actions) that comes out of your life and mouth.

4) You will live on a solid foundation. You will be certain that your life will never crumble, because the Lord holds you up at all times.

Are these descriptions true of your life? Pick one to work on this week.

tuesday Luke 7:1-10

Digging Deeper • A centurion is a soldier in the Roman army—an enemy of the Jews. But this man was not a typical centurion. Not only did he care for Jews (giving the Jews a place of worship), but this centurion even cared about his servants, who usually weren't considered that important. The most remarkable thing about this centurion, though, was that he had faith that Christ could do anything, anywhere, in anyone's life. His faith was so remarkable that even Jesus made mention of it as an example for others to follow. His faith was richly rewarded reminding us that it pays to believe and obey.

Do you really believe that God is powerful enough to take care of all your problems? Are there any situations where you do not trust Him right now?

wednesday Luke 7:11-23

Digging Deeper • Today's miracle happened with no preparation at all—that is, no one even asked Jesus to help. His heart was simply moved to help someone in distress. We need to be just as sensitive to people around us. Why wait to help in church, or until we are asked? We can't raise people from the dead, but God doesn't ask us to do that. He just wants us to serve one another in love (Galatians 5:13). Jesus also showed love by affirming Who He was for John the Baptist, who was in prison and about to die. Jesus was the Messiah because He had fulfilled the prophecies, such as doing miracles, and John could be encouraged to know that his life's work in preparing for the Messiah had come to fruition.

Are you ready to serve at any moment? Whom can you serve today without being asked?

thursday Luke 7:24-35

Digging Deeper • John the Baptist *was* a good speaker, and he *was* humble, but perhaps you thought he was just another guy in the Bible. Imagine having Jesus say verse 28 about you! Jesus points out to John's messengers that the Pharisees missed God's purpose for themselves. The Pharisees had the perfect messages from the great men, but they still refused to believe. They labeled both Jesus and John incorrectly (vv. 33-34). But any wise person could see that Jesus and John were from God. Greatness is not always popular, and sometimes it is even difficult. Have you ever been labeled falsely? You're in good company with Jesus and John the Baptist.

Are you willing to be labeled incorrectly for Jesus' sake? Are you seeking to be great by the world's standards, or God's?

friday   Luke 7:36-50

Digging Deeper • We're not sure why this Pharisee wanted Jesus in his home, because most of the Pharisees wanted nothing to do with Jesus. In contrast, this woman chose to come and sit at Jesus' feet. Jesus' story showed the difference between the woman's attitude toward Jesus, and Simon's (the Pharisee's) attitude. The woman understood that Jesus had forgiven many of her sins, and that's why she loved Him so much. The Pharisee didn't consider himself very sinful, and as a result he didn't love Jesus much. He didn't understand the fundamental part of salvation—that we are all horrible sinners.

How do you view yourself, and the sins you've committed? Do you love Jesus more because of all His forgiveness toward you and your wrong? How does this affect your actions?

saturday   Luke 8:1-15

Digging Deeper • In today's parable we need to understand that Jesus is teaching hundreds of people. He describes four heart attitudes when receiving God's Word (vv. 11-14), and He represents them with different kinds of soil. This was a great example because everyone knew what it was like to grow things in good or poor soil. Jesus' use of parables separated those people who were there to see a miracle from those who genuinely wanted to hear and understand God's Word. Even if they didn't understand the story, they could ask questions and find out the truth. Unfortunately, some just walked away.

How great is your passion to understand God's Word? Do you give up, or do you ask God to help you? How about asking those who know God's Word better than you to give you a hand?

Week 21

Being a follower of Jesus is not an easy road! We may think that pastors and missionaries are great people, but greatness may take them through some very challenging lessons. Watch the disciples learn some of these lessons, and be careful to practice them yourself.

prayer focus for this week

 the Question

 the Answer

What is the writer saying?

How can I apply this to my life?

sunday   Luke 8:16-25

Q

A

Digging Deeper • Jesus continues teaching His Word and emphasizing the necessity of putting it into practice. In today's passage, He does so in three ways: (1) Jesus shares that God wants to reveal light (His Word) to everyone so all can benefit from it. The challenge for us is in verse 18. We must be careful and attentive when we listen to His Word, and God will add to our understanding. (2) He uses the teachable moment to share that Jesus is deeply connected (like relationships within a family) with anyone that puts His Word into practice. (3) Lastly, He gives a special object lesson just for His disciples. Jesus told them they would go to the other side of the lake, but the disciples thought they were going to drown. They forgot Who they were with and didn't take Jesus at His word.

What is one specific area in which you can practice God's Word better?

monday Luke 8:26-40

Digging Deeper • Understand that the demon called himself "Legion" because a *legion* was a term used to describe up to 6,000 Roman soldiers. The man was possessed by many demons. We see two very different responses to Jesus' healing: (1) One healed person was changed in appearance and wanted to be at Jesus' feet. He told everyone he could about the Lord and His grace. (2) The others were afraid of Jesus. Why? They were afraid of truth. Learning something that requires you to change can put you in a tough spot sometimes. Often God wants you to do something difficult, but the healed man would never have wanted it any different. The Truth (Jesus) actually sets us free!

Is there something in your life that you're afraid to change? How can you trust Jesus today in learning a difficult lesson, in order to be closer to Him?

tuesday Luke 8:41-56

Digging Deeper • We see two miracles today—both with the same lesson of faith. The lady who touched Jesus believed that if she could only touch Him, she would be healed, even if she were sneaky about it. The other example of faith was Jairus, who refused to be swayed by his friends (v. 49) or the people at his house (v. 53). He did as Jesus said and reaped the benefit. God's great work in our lives is limited only by our own obedience. He wants to do great things *for* us and *through* us, *in perfect accordance with His will*.

Who do you trust more than anyone else—God or your friends? Do you listen to God's words more than to your friends'?

wednesday Luke 9:1-11

Digging Deeper • Jesus sent out His twelve disciples with the ability to do great miracles and preach the Gospel. The key was to preach the Gospel; the miracles merely helped show people they were speaking God's Word. Next, we read about Herod, who had John the Baptist beheaded. John was a great man, and obviously Herod was a little nervous that his evil act was coming back to haunt him. That's what unconfessed sin does to anyone—Christian or non-Christian. They live a life of fear instead of peace. Peace comes when you know you're forgiven, and you can start every day fresh and in perfect fellowship with Jesus.

Are you afraid someone may find out something that you did wrong? Will you confess it to God and the people you've hidden it from?

thursday Luke 9:12-22

Digging Deeper • Where would the disciples get food to feed 5,000 people? The same place Jesus did. He wanted to see if they had the faith to trust God for it. When they didn't have the same trust, Jesus gave them a great reminder with this lesson. One basket of food was left over for each of the doubting disciples. In the next few verses, it appears Peter was beginning to learn. He didn't listen to the crowds like others, such as Herod (Luke 9:8-9) had (v. 19). Peter knew who Jesus was, and as a result, the Lord would use Peter in great ways in the future. In fact, Jesus gives him the first hint of His betrayal, death, and resurrection in verses 21 and 22—perhaps to help Peter remember his bold stand here.

How do you doubt Jesus? Have you learned from your past mistakes? How will your increased faith help you in trials in the future?

friday · Luke 9:23-36

Digging Deeper • These three disciples were especially blessed to get to see Jesus like this. In verse 27, Jesus wasn't referring to Heaven when He said the "kingdom of God"; He was talking about Himself. One reason Peter, James, and John saw Jesus in all His glory was so they would not be ashamed of knowing Christ and standing up for Him (v. 26). The key is verse 23—the mark of a Christian who has been saved by Christ and will one day see Him in His full glory is that Christian's actions—taking up Christ's cross and following Him.

Are you willing to deny yourself of what you want to live for Christ? Have you seen Christ enough—in getting to know Him every day—that you are not ashamed to stand up for Him? How can you follow Christ and see Him today?

saturday · Luke 9:37-50

Digging Deeper • Was Jesus mean to this man in verse 41? Not at all. We often look at pastors and missionaries as great people. We want to do great things for God like they do. Jesus helps people understand that greatness doesn't come by doing the miracles. Greatness is a life of humility and a challenging road. Jesus didn't want His disciples to marvel at the miracles anymore—His challenging road of greatness was going to lead Him to betrayal and death! The disciples were still trying to show how *great* they were by doing miracles. Jesus stops the disciples' quarrel and tells them to humble themselves like a little child. Humility and being "the least" is greatness.

Do you try to show people how great you are with the things you are good at? How are you going to humble yourself today?

Jesus begins to head toward His death, but His teaching is far from over. He really focuses on the key elements in the Christian walk this week. This is a great week to challenge yourself and re-examine your heart with the fundamental teachings of Christ.

prayer focus for this week

the Question What is the writer saying?

the Answer How can I apply this to my life?

sunday Luke 9:51-62

Q

A

Digging Deeper • The key transition in Jesus' life was the day He headed for Jerusalem. After three years of traveling through Israel's countryside, healing and ministering, He turned toward the city of His death, as He had predicted to His disciples. Verse 51 describes His attitude: a resolve to do it, a steadfast decision. As He walked, He passed on the challenge to others. A life of sacrifice and commitment to God's work is not always convenient, but we should never look back. We need to constantly press ahead to do the Father's will for us, looking to be carried through on strength from God rather than the things of this earth. Christ was not even guaranteed physical comforts (vv. 58-62).

How focused are you at doing God's will no matter the cost? What area do you need to resolve to follow God in right now?

monday Luke 10:1-12

Digging Deeper • Jesus sent out 70 disciples to heal the sick, and to tell them that Jesus, Himself would be coming through that way. Jesus told His disciples that God's workers are few. Many people need to hear Christ, and even want to, but there are so few who are willing to go and tell them. We are to pray that God will send people out, and we also need to be willing to go ourselves. Jesus gave His disciples instruction on being well received as well as being rejected. Even though many would turn them away, Jesus told them to still go. Our job today is to share the Gospel. People may not accept it, but we still need to go and leave the rest to God. Evangelism is our job; conversion is His!

Have you ever considered being a full-time missionary or pastor? Before you finish your Quiet Time, will you ask the Lord to send people out?

tuesday Luke 10:13-24

Digging Deeper • Jesus pronounces "woes" on some cities that didn't respond well to His truth, even after seeing much of the Lord. This implies that there could be degrees of punishment in Hell. Also, the disciples were joyful that the demons submitted to them, but Jesus said they shouldn't take joy in that because God gave them the power over the demons in the first place. Also, simply being saved and children of God is enough. No matter how talented or gifted we are, our salvation should be sufficient for all the joy we need.

What really makes you joyful? Is it possessions, popularity, friends, or simply Christ? When was the last time you prayed and didn't ask God for anything, but were just thankful to Him for saving you?

wednesday Luke 10:25-37

Digging Deeper • A sign of someone who has successfully "inherited salvation" is a love for God and others. That is why Jesus asked the man how he read the law—to get to his heart. When it came to loving his neighbor, this man tried to redefine God's Word by not saying everybody was his neighbor. But in the story Jesus told, the person who helped the man who was robbed was not his neighbor—one was a Jew; one was a Samaritan, and Jews hated Samaritans. Jesus wanted the man to have God's perspective—loving the world — instead of man's perspective, which involves the sinful effects of only loving those whom we choose to.

Who is someone you know who most people choose not to love, and how can you show God's love to them today?

thursday Luke 10:38-42

Digging Deeper • Both Mary and Martha were doing good things. Martha was serving the Lord because He was a guest in her house. What could be wrong with that? It's wonderful to do good things for the Lord, but if it ever gets in the way of sitting at Jesus' feet, and building your relationship with Him, it can be wrong. It was more important to just be with Jesus. Jesus said only "one" thing is needed. Your first priority in life will always be to build your relationship with Him. We can never allow school, church work, jobs, sports, friends, or other good things that we think will please God to be first. It's not that we don't do these other things, but our relationship with Jesus must always come first.

What takes the place of your relationship with Christ? What are you going to do to make Him first?

friday　Luke 11:1-13

Digging Deeper • Jesus teaches His disciples to pray. One of the key elements before we ask the Lord for anything is for us to desire *His* will to be done, not *ours*! Jesus then taught His disciples the importance of asking God for His grace in life. The only way to hear "yes" to a prayer is to ask! The Lord wants us to be bold as we ask; always remembering that it's what God wants that is most important. Once we ask, we then allow God to do what is best, and often He will bless our request. Sometimes people see God as holding a big rubber stamp that says "NO" on it. That's not true! Verses 9-13 are the Father's wonderful expression of how He wants to bless our lives.

When you ask, is your will always submitted to God's? What specific need can you pray for today? Are you willing to accept any answer from God?

saturday　Luke 11:14-28

Digging Deeper • Jesus was accused of driving out demons by Satan's power before. He asked why, if Satan took hold of someone in the first place, would he then give the power to release him? Satan has a battle plan, and he isn't going to stand against himself, so when Jesus drove out demons, it could only be by God's power. Jesus then points out that after all the miracles He did, the people still just wanted to see more and not change their hearts. Jesus tells them the final sign would be the three days before He came out of the grave, a parallel to Jonah, who was in the belly of a fish for three days and three nights. But the people's hearts were hard, and they would not believe Jesus' previous miracles or in the ultimate miracle to come.

Take a moment to thank God for miracles and the miracle of your salvation.

Hypocrisy hurts the church. Jesus despised hypocrisy while He lived on this earth, and He still despises it today. Check out this week's passages and you'll see hypocrisy at its worst—but you'll also see instructions from Christ on how to live in a genuine way.

prayer focus for this week

the Question

the Answer

What is the writer saying?

How can I apply this to my life?

sunday   Luke 11:29-41

Digging Deeper • We are a nation obsessed with purity in many ways. We want to drink pure water, breathe pure air, and eat pure foods. Yet there is one area where purity doesn't seem to be important to us—the heart. We are much more concerned with clean hands than clean hearts. The Pharisees (which, by the way, were the most religious people of their day) were also more concerned with the outside than the inside. Check out Psalm 24:3-6. What are a couple other signs of a person who has a clean heart? How is this person different than the Pharisees you read about today? Those in the presence of God must be pure inside.

What do you pay more attention to—what people think of you, or whether your heart pleases God? Is there anything in your life that resembles a Pharisee or a person with an unclean heart?

monday Luke 11:42-54

Digging Deeper • Have you ever thought about what Jesus might say to you if He were to drop by for a visit in the middle of your youth group meeting? His words might not be so pretty. He might address the fact that much of our Christianity is surface in nature. Can you see the harshness of Jesus' words as He spoke to the Pharisees in this passage? Jesus let them have it—He didn't hold back. He reprimanded them for putting so much emphasis on the external and adding their own traditions to the Word of God. The church today has a tendency to do that as well. We must guard ourselves from this desire to add things to the Scripture that just aren't there.
Would Jesus label you a hypocrite? Is your Christianity sincere, or do you just do things for God when it easy or convenient?

tuesday Luke 12:1-15

Digging Deeper • Did you know that you are important to God? While Jesus again speaks to the Pharisees about hypocrisy, He transitions with some beautiful statements about God's love for us. The harsh tone becomes an encouraging and comforting one. Jesus assures us of how important we are to the Father. In fact, as Jesus talks about his Father's love for the insignificant sparrow, He emphasizes that we are much more important than some mere bird. He says His Father knows us so intimately that He even knows how many hairs we have on our heads! The bottom line is that God loves us, and we are important to Him.
Isn't it encouraging knowing that God thinks you're important? Look for examples today of how God is providing for you, and think of ways to thank Him for that.

Wednesday Luke 12:16-34

Digging Deeper • Do you ever get consumed with yourself or wrapped up in your circumstances? Do you forget that other people are on this planet with you? If so, then take a lesson from our passage today. It's easy to become self-obsessed when the culture tells you to look out for number one. Jesus often used parables when He taught, and in this particular instance, He speaks of a rich man who was consumed with himself. His words to the man shoot straight to the heart. He clearly emphasizes that it's more important to be kingdom-focused than self-focused.
Are you kingdom-focused? What are you doing to help the kingdom of God? What are some areas where you could be less self-focused?

thursday Luke 12:35-48

Digging Deeper • Are you ready for Christ's return? If not, the message here is clear: Get ready. Be on your toes. Watch! Although there are some who debate which future event this passage is referring to, the principle applies to us today. Jesus urges us to be ready. Don't keep doing what you've been doing. Repent of your sins, and live like today could be your last. Some practical ways you could do this are to share your faith with that person you've been hesitant to share with, or take time to do that extra Bible study or reading you know you should be doing instead of putting it off until next year. Be faithful in your church attendance. Take time to pray rather than burning time watching TV or browsing the Internet. You never know what tomorrow (much less today) holds.
What if Jesus came back tonight? What would He find you doing?

friday Luke 12:49-59

Digging Deeper • Do you believe that Jesus is the only way to Heaven, even if that belief may not be popular among your circle of friends? The claim that Christ is the only way to Heaven often brings opposition and hatred. However, we shouldn't be surprised. Jesus said that true Christianity brings division, not global peace. After Jesus makes this initial point, He talks about the weather for a minute. He does this not to give a forecast (though He is more qualified than your local weatherman), but to make a point. His point is that while man is intelligent in many ways (the weather), he is often ignorant about what matters most (spiritual matters). **Who can you talk to today about spiritual matters—what matters most? How much time do you spend talking about trivial matters, and how can you turn those conversations to Christ?**

saturday Luke 13:1-9

Digging Deeper • All great teachers do their best to relate to their audience using whatever means they can to get their attention. In our passage today, Jesus mentions two current events (vv. 2-4). One of the points that He makes in verse 4 is that not everything bad that happens to someone is some kind of divine punishment. While sometimes God punishes us due to our sin (see Hebrews 12:5-11), oftentimes the difficulties are just a part of the maturing process that we go through as Christians. We need to be careful not to judge others so quickly, and accuse them of being horrible sinners, when the difficulty in their lives may not be divine discipline, but merely temporary trials (see James 1:2-4). **How often do you assume that people's hard times are because of their behavior? How can you instead reach out and show them Christ's love?**

Jesus was a great storyteller. He didn't tell stories to get a crowd, but to make spiritual applications. In our passages this week, we'll come face to face with some of His most beloved stories that have impacted people throughout the centuries.

prayer focus for this week

the **Question**
the **Answer**

What is the writer saying?

How can I apply this to my life?

sunday   Luke 13:10-21

Digging Deeper • Aren't you glad to serve a God whose main focus is your relationship with Him? In this passage, we notice a crippled woman who had not stood up straight in 18 years. Jesus did what He did many times on the Sabbath day and healed this woman. The religious leaders, however, considered this to be work, which was a *no-no* on the Sabbath Day. Isn't it incredibly selfish that these religious people were more concerned with the fact that one of their rules had been broken than that this woman, who'd been afflicted for 18 years, experienced true physical healing? They were so caught up in the rules that they probably didn't even notice this woman's appropriate response to the healing: she "glorified God!"

When is the last time God did something amazing in your life? Did you thank Him for it? How can you show concern for people's needs today?

monday   Luke 13:22-35

Digging Deeper • This passage talks about the coming day of judgment. Many will claim that they have done enough good to get into Heaven, arguing that surely, they *must* be saved. But the response of Jesus shows that they were professors (saying they knew God) only and not possessors (really knowing God). Their false testimonies made them "workers of iniquity." This is a scary thought and one that should cause us to examine our own conversion to make sure we're ready for the day when we stand before Jesus Christ Himself.

What will you say when it is time to say why you should be allowed into Heaven? Is your salvation something you merely talk about, or maybe something you associate with your family? Or can you say without a doubt that you "know" God (vv. 25-27)? What can you do about that today?

tuesday   Luke 14:1-14

Digging Deeper • In today's passage, Jesus takes time to eat lunch with some Pharisees. Usually He put these showy religious leaders in their place with His answers to their trick questions, but on this occasion, He accepts the offer and has a meal with them. It's interesting to note that Jesus took the time to heal a man at this meal, as well as rebuke the Pharisees once again for their warped views. But after He finishes this miracle, He also takes some time to talk about pride and humility. In a nutshell, Jesus explains that pride is thinking of yourself first while humility is thinking of yourself last.

When was the last time you did something for someone with no thought of what they could do for you? Who could you put first today?

wednesday Luke 14:15-24

Digging Deeper • Jesus expresses some frustration in this parable. He tells the story of a man preparing a great feast for the sole purpose of inviting others to eat with him. Unfortunately, after the supper was prepared, and the people were invited to come, the excuses came from everywhere. One had an estate problem he had to take care of. Another had animals to test drive, and still another needed to talk to his wife. None of these things were bad in and of themselves, but they became hindrances to accepting the invitation. That's the way it is today concerning the great invitation that Jesus offers. All that needs to be done to get people saved has been done, but people still delay and spend their time on earthly concerns.
What keeps the people you know from accepting Christ? How can you use these verses to show them the importance of seeking Christ today?

thursday Luke 14:25-35

Digging Deeper • When you were growing up, did you ever use the word *hate*? Often, parents try to keep their kids from using the word because of its extremely negative meaning. But as Jesus uses the word *hate* here, while it is severe, we should understand it in its relative sense. He doesn't mean we should literally hate our parents, our siblings, and those individuals closest to us. That's not the point at all. The point is, compared to our love for the Lord, all of our love for others should seem as hate. We should be so focused on following Him that allegiances to others fall and fade into a distant second place.
How much do you love the Lord? Does your attachment to earthly things— whether it be family members or other interests—ever keep you from serving Christ with all you have?

friday   Luke 15:1-10

Digging Deeper • Have you ever thought of Jesus as a shepherd? In our passage today, Jesus is seen taking care of sheep, but more specifically, looking for one lost sheep. This parable emphasizes that despite the fact that He knows where ninety-nine of His one hundred sheep are (a good percentage, right?), He searches for His one lost sheep until He finds it. He never gives up. After He finally finds this one, He celebrates its homecoming by throwing a party. Jesus is still looking for lost sheep today. He is seeking those that don't know Him or who have strayed from Him. When one is found, the results are the same: celebration, excitement, and rejoicing.
Did you realize that God threw a party when you became a Christian? What are you doing to make sure others come to know Jesus Christ?

saturday   Luke 15:11-32

Digging Deeper • Jesus has always been and will always be in the business of saving the lost. Today's passage about the prodigal son is similar to yesterday's verses, concerning the one lost sheep. In the parable, the father waits for his lost son—he is even outside waiting for him to come home! Once he arrives the father gives his once *lost* son new clothes, new shoes, and literally, a new life. So many of us have left God's blessings and tried to find happiness on our own, but even as we reject God's love, He is waiting for us to come back so He can bless us more.
How has God been good to you, in spite of your past? How can you thank Him for His faithfulness today? How can you tell others that God is still waiting for them to come back?

Jesus was never afraid to be straight up. We never see Him trying to tiptoe around certain subjects. In this week's passages, we'll see Him addressing such controversial topics as money, divorce, and Hell.

prayer focus for this week

the Question — What is the writer saying?

the Answer — How can I apply this to my life?

sunday   Luke 16:1-18

Q

A

Digging Deeper • Who wants to be a millionaire? Almost everyone I know does, but is that what we should be concerned with? Certainly, it's not wrong to have money, but it is wrong for money to have you. After all, no man can serve both God and money (mammon—v. 13), can he? The obvious answer—and the one Jesus supplied—was, "No, it is impossible to serve both God and stuff." Way too many people buy things that they don't really need, with money they may not have, to impress people or make themselves feel good. God is not pleased with that. Invest in what really matters. Remember that you are pleasing Jesus when you give.
Is money an idol in your life? Make a list of the last five things you spent money on. Would your purchases or giving please Jesus?

monday　Luke 16:19-31

Digging Deeper • Smoking or non-smoking? When it comes to restaurants, that is the choice we're often confronted with as we enter the doors. The truth is, we're confronted with a similar, though far more significant choice, when it comes to eternity. That choice is Heaven or Hell. While it's not pleasant to think of an actual place called Hell, that doesn't make it any less real (just like trying to pretend algebra doesn't exist won't keep you from having to go to class). The truth is that when you die, you will spend eternity in one of two places: Heaven or Hell. As you read Jesus' story about the rich man and Lazarus, realize that you have a choice to make (if you haven't done so already), and it's eternally more important than some seating section in a restaurant.

Do you believe in a real Heaven and Hell? How does this affect your life?

tuesday　Luke 17:1-19

Digging Deeper • In today's passage, we see ten lepers who were healed, but only one of them showed his thanks to God. Notice that verse 16 says he was a Samaritan, meaning that although he was not part of God's "chosen people," he still received God's blessing. This man realized he had done nothing to receive healing, and he was truly thankful for it. Too often, though, we expect blessings from God and therefore aren't as thankful as we should be when he does something amazing for us. In verses 17-18, we can see that Jesus noticed who was grateful; we can be sure He will see our thankfulness, too.

What are some things that you expect God to automatically give you? Do you take time to thank Him for these blessings? What can you thank God for today?

wednesday Luke 17:20-37

Digging Deeper • Revelation. Rapture. Second Coming. Do these words scare you? They can be intimidating. Sometimes we feel like we have enough trouble with the present to be worried about the future. But Jesus says that the future is important, and we need to think about it! One thing we can know is that Christ is coming again. In this passage, Christ is talking about the taking of those who have not placed their faith in Christ, not the Rapture (when Jesus comes in the sky and takes believers with Him to Heaven—1 Thessalonians 4:16-17). These verses refer to Christ coming to the earth a second time. This time He will be coming to judge those who have not trusted in Him as their Savior.
Are you prepared for the future? If not, what will you do to be sure you're ready for Christ?

thursday Luke 18:1-14

Digging Deeper • Do you know anyone who is persistent? They'll keep asking for what they want until they finally get it, much like the woman found in our passage today. She continually approaches this judge, insisting on being avenged. Scripture does not tell us her specific problem, but day, after day, after day, she persisted in seeking the verdict that she wanted from this judge. In the end, she got it. The application for us is that persistence in prayer is rewarded. We are urged not to give up, but to keep asking God, never ceasing in our prayer.
Do you pray with the persistence of this woman? Have you ever quit praying about something because you felt God would never answer?

fRiday   Luke 18:15-27

Digging Deeper • "Jesus Loves the Little Children" is more than a children's song. It's the truth. We see this in our passage today. When the disciples tried to keep children away from Jesus, He told them to let the children come (v. 16). Jesus saw the children as He sees all people—individuals who need to come to Him to be saved. In fact, Jesus said these children had an advantage, in that they knew how to approach God in faith (v. 17)—unlike others, who may be held back by their position or possessions (vv. 24-25).

If you were a Christian when you were a child, what was your faith in Christ like then? How are your possessions or your status among people keeping you from having complete faith in Him today?

saturday   Luke 18:28-43

Digging Deeper • Do you believe that God still does miracles? He may operate differently in our day and age, but He still does amazing things. In our passage, we see the account of the healing of a blind man, who is known in the other gospels as Bartimaeus. In this story, Bartimaeus hears a lot of commotion going on and asks about it. When he finds out that Jesus is approaching, he calls out to Him, begging for Him to do a miracle in his life. Jesus, with great compassion and amazement at his faith, chooses to heal him. This leads to thanks from Bartimaeus and amazement by all those who witnessed it. God still does miracles today—He has forgiven your sins and given you eternal life.

Who in your life needs to come to Christ? Do you believe that Jesus can change their life?

Jesus knew the time of His death was approaching, but He continued to minister to all types of people—even those who didn't like Him! This week, see how Jesus *gets to the heart*—He sees people's motives and whether they are really serving Him, no matter what they look like on the outside.

prayer focus for this week

the Question the Answer

What is the writer saying?

How can I apply this to my life?

sunday Luke 19:1-10

Digging Deeper • Zacchaeus was a tax collector, a job known for dishonesty and manipulation. Despite his reputation, though, he was a man who wanted to see Jesus. Since he couldn't see over or get through the crowd surrounding Jesus because of his height, he climbed a tree and waited for a glimpse of Him. Jesus also wanted to see Zacchaeus, and as a result of meeting Jesus that day, Zacchaeus' life was changed forever. That change is manifested by what he was willing to do.

Have you experienced Jesus firsthand? How was your life changed by the encounter? What effort will you make to spend time with Him today?

monday Luke 19:11-27

Digging Deeper • Faithfulness is almost always rewarded, but laziness rarely is. Jesus' parable in our passage today illustrates that point perfectly. Faithfully use what God has given you. If He has blessed you financially, invest in the work of the church. If He has blessed you physically, do all you can with your body until it's worn out. If He has blessed you musically, sing or play an instrument to the glory of God. But whatever you do, don't sit back and do nothing with your gifts. God has been gracious to give you your personality, natural abilities, spiritual gifts, and various life experiences. You can thank Him by investing in the kingdom of God.

Name some areas in which you know you are gifted. Where and how do you regularly use these? What have you done with what God has given you?

tuesday Luke 19:28-44

Digging Deeper • Many of Jesus' followers were excited about Jesus entering the city as their king. In verse 37, the people praised God for what they had seen Jesus do, and now they were anticipating Him doing great things in the future. They didn't understand that before He would be king, He had to suffer and die for His subjects. As Jesus saw the city, He cried. He was sorrowful for those that had rejected Him and not accepted Him. They would have to suffer for many years before they would come to repentance and finally be ruled by the true, loving, and powerful King. Only days later the Pharisees and many of the people of the city would be shouting "Crucify Him!"

What do you feel for those that reject Jesus as Lord and Savior? Ask the Lord to help you feel for people the way He does.

wednesday Luke 19:45 - 20:8

Digging Deeper • Is it ever appropriate to be angry? The answer is yes! We are told to be angry, but sin not. An infusion of anger might be the very thing the church needs. It should be angry with the forces of evil, angry at pornography that reaches into every segment of society, angry at the abuse of drugs and alcohol in our society, angry because there are millions of people who are dying without Christ, and angry at our own sinful habits! The truth is, anger at sin isn't always sinful. In the Old Testament, there are over 375 references to God the Father being angry. And obviously, in our passage today, we see Jesus getting angry, but only at the right times and for the right reasons. Anger is not always sinful, sometimes anger is even necessary to push us toward treating sin the way we should.

What have you been tolerating that you need to get angry about?

thursday Luke 20:9-26

Digging Deeper • Do you have any enemies? Are there people in your life who simply hate you? If so, you're like Jesus in some ways, because Jesus sure had his share of enemies. What is most surprising about Jesus' enemies is that they were the most religious people of His day. They knew the most Scripture verses and kept the law the best. Jesus is addressing His enemies in our passage today. As was His custom, Jesus used a story to describe this hatred that the religious people had for Him. Ultimately, He tells the religious leaders and the rest of the crowd that there will be those who hate and oppose God so much that they will kill His very own Son.

How does Christ's attitude toward His enemies show you how to react to those who hate God and the things and people of God?

friday   Luke 20:27-38

Digging Deeper • Can God make a rock so big that even He can't pick up? Where did they put the woodpeckers and termites on the ark? Who did Cain marry? For years, unbelievers and agnostics have been asking trick questions, trying to put down Christianity and discredit the Bible. Even in Jesus' day there were those who opposed the faith with these types of questions. But Jesus never flinched. He made it clear that what was important was not the answer to these trivia questions, but the fact that there would one day be a real resurrection. In the midst of a crazy question about Heaven, Jesus tells us that we can be sure that the dead will be raised to life one day, and that Heaven does indeed exist.

When people try to discredit Christ and the truth, how can you get to the heart of the issue and share valuable wisdom with them?

saturday   Luke 20:39 - 21:4

Digging Deeper • God is concerned with *why* we do things as much as He's concerned with *what* we do. He looks at our motives and with our actions because it is possible to do good things with wrong motives. In this passage, He points out the hypocritical lifestyle of some people, such as how they pray and give. Do you ever pray in a certain way because you want others to say "Wow!" at how spiritual you sounded? Do you do it so others will see that you're putting something in the offering plate? The truth is that God knows everything, and He sees beyond your actions. He sees your motives. You should look at your motives, too, to see whether your actions are really pleasing God.

Why do you give? Is it for show? How about why you pray? How will you examine your motives today?

Week 27

Who would you spend time with, and what would you say to them if you knew your last days on earth were approaching? This week, we get a glimpse into how Jesus spent His last days on earth.

prayer focus for this week

the Question   What is the writer saying?
the Answer   How can I apply this to my life?

sunday   Luke 21:5-19

Digging Deeper • What is your faith costing you? I've noticed that many people today have an *air-conditioned* faith. In other words, they have a faith that is convenient. Their life runs on one track, with them fitting time with God or church activities in the cracks. And so their Christianity is casual at best. Yes, it is true that most of our lives will never be threatened for us being Christians, but that shouldn't make us comfortable—it should make us thankful instead. More than that, we should be determined to take advantage of the freedoms that we have. Let's make Christ our priority and not be satisfied with a *comfortable* Christian life. Let's share our faith in spite of the little bit of ridicule and rejection we may possibly face.

When is the last time you did something hard for Christ or another person? Are you taking advantage of the freedom you have to share Christ?

monday   Luke 21:20-38

Digging Deeper • Are things getting better or worse here on earth? Many people want to think that things are getting better. But this passage teaches that things are going to get worse in the world before Jesus comes, and only when He comes will terrible events end. While this isn't easy to think about, we have hope because we know God is in control and that He has a wonderful plan for those who love and trust in Him. Despite the troubles in the world, as His children, we can rest assured that we are in good hands. We may not know what the future holds, but we know Who holds the future!

How are you trusting in the Lord for your future? How can you share your hope for the future with others?

tuesday   Luke 22:1-20

Digging Deeper • The Lord's Supper. The Eucharist. Communion. It has many names, but what is important is what happens during this special time, which was started by Jesus. In our passage today, we see Jesus instituting the Lord's Supper (see 1 Corinthians 11 for more details). During the Lord's Supper, there should be a time when we *look backward* and think about all that Christ did for us on the cross by taking our place and paying our sin debt. There should be a time when we *look inward*, examining our personal relationship with Christ. And finally, there should be a *forward look*, as any day now we can expect Christ to return for us.

When you partake of the Lord's Supper, do you take it seriously? Are you taking the proper *looks* in observing the Lord's Supper?

wednesday Luke 22:21-38

Digging Deeper • What is the recipe for greatness in God's kingdom? Are there certain things you must accomplish to be considered great in God's sight? These are the kinds of questions that the disciples were asking Jesus. As only Jesus can, He makes things very clear by saying that if you want to be great in God's kingdom, you must be willing to do the little things. In other words, to be considered great in God's kingdom today may involve mopping floors, washing dishes, or even taking out the trash. Doesn't sound so *great*, does it? Yet Jesus says this is what greatness is all about—servanthood.

Are you pursuing the kind of greatness that Jesus spoke of? Are you willing to do the little acts of service that no one else wants to do? What kind of *little things* can you do this week to help someone else out?

thursday Luke 22:39-53

Digging Deeper • Have you ever heard someone say, "The anticipation is killing me!"? Usually, they're exaggerating. But in Jesus' case, as He approaches the day of his crucifixion, He prays a very real prayer. The anticipation of the cross is beginning to take its toll. He is not exaggerating in the least when He says, "Father, if thou be willing, remove this cup from me." Some feel that He knew what had to be done but was perhaps asking God for more time to win the lost; others feel that He was speaking from a human standpoint and just asking to avoid the suffering if there was any other way salvation could be brought. Above all, though, Jesus just wanted God's will to be done no matter what it might cost Him!

Can you say in the midst of tough decisions, "Not my will, but yours!"?

friday Luke 22:54-71

Digging Deeper • Jesus is God. It's something He never denied, even in the face of death. As you read the gospels, it seems rather obvious that these claims to be God didn't help His reputation among the religious leaders of His day. In fact, they were more than a little outraged about His claim to be God. They knew well what He was claiming, and they considered it blasphemy (which it would have been, if He wasn't really God). If you haven't recognized Jesus as the God of your life, go back through the words and miracles of Christ. See if it's time to say that this Jesus really was—and is—God.

Have you come to the place in your life where you've recognized Jesus as God in the flesh? If not, what are you waiting for?

saturday Luke 23:1-12

Digging Deeper • Who was Jesus to Pilate? As Jesus stood before Pilate, one can't help but wonder what was going through Pilate's mind. Was he nervous? Did he have any inkling at all that this really could be the Son of God? Or was it business as usual? We don't really know what Pilate was thinking, but we know that he questioned Jesus but could find no faults (vv. 3-4). In the end, history doesn't tell us if Pilate ever came to know Jesus as his personal Savior, but we do know he let others condemn Jesus, even when he could find nothing wrong with Him. He ignored the testimony of Christ. Instead of finding out more about this faultless Man, Jesus, he let the crowd decide His fate.

Who is Jesus to you? That's the most important decision you will ever make in your life because it will determine your eternity.

Week 28

The death and resurrection of Jesus Christ shows a lot about not only Jesus but also the normal, sinful humans who were closest to him. As we watch Christ make the ultimate sacrifice for humanity, keep an eye on those around Him for lessons on how to act and *not* act, both in bad and good times.

prayer focus for this week

the Question
the Answer

What is the writer saying?

How can I apply this to my life?

sunday Luke 23:13-25

Digging Deeper • Have you ever blown it big time? Have you ever been confronted with a choice, and not only made the wrong choice, but really did something dumb? Sure you have. You're just like everyone else—you're human! We've all blown it! The Bible affirms this truth (Romans 3:23). In our passage today, Pilate makes a horrible mistake and releases a murderer while sentencing Jesus to death by crucifixion. Pilate blew it. He thought he was through with Christ when he sent Him to Herod, but the truth was, he was given a second chance to recognize Jesus for Who He truly was, the Son of God. And what did he do with that opportunity? He made another huge mistake.

Aren't you glad God gives second chances? Who can you pray for or talk to this week so that they won't blow a second chance?

monday Luke 23:26-43

Digging Deeper • Have you ever forgiven someone who has never even asked for your forgiveness? As in so many cases, Jesus Himself is our example. From the cross, He said several different things, but the most interesting was when He prayed, "Father, forgive them, for they know not what they do." Wow, what an amazing attitude! And yet we can't even get over that classmate who said something nasty about us! Why don't we take some time to really learn something from Jesus' example today, and forgive someone who has hurt us.

Who do you need to forgive despite the fact that they've never asked for your forgiveness? How can you look at life with a forgiving attitude—accepting how people have hurt you and choosing to love them rather than retaliating?

tuesday Luke 23:44-56

Digging Deeper • When someone who has influenced many lives dies, there are a variety of ways that people react. In this passage, we can see humanity's initial reaction to the death of its Savior. The physical earth experienced turmoil (v. 44); the place of worship fell before a new Intercessor (v. 45); a Roman soldier realized he was looking at true righteousness (v. 47); the crowds reacted to their deed finally being done (v. 48); a righteous man served His God (vv. 50-53); and Jesus' faithful servants gave to Him the best they could (vv. 55-56).

When you think of the crucifixion and all that Jesus did for you on the cross, what kind of emotions do you feel? While Christ's death—and any attacks against Him today—are praised by those who hate Him, His selflessness and forgiveness should spur us to thankfulness and service.

wednesday Luke 24:1-12

Digging Deeper • Jesus is alive! This is one of the most important truths in all of Scripture. When we read the words, "He is not here, but is risen," we should get excited. Since Jesus is alive and well, our lives can now be different. We can have peace in our lives and hope for our future. We can live every day with joy in our hearts. What would your life be like if Jesus did not rise from the dead? It would be pointless, meaningless, and a waste—a constant fight against doing what isn't right, which would only hurt you and others. But we can rejoice, because He is alive and well. Because He lives, we live also!

How should Jesus being alive affect your life and your attitude?

thursday Luke 24:13-27

Digging Deeper • Would you recognize Jesus if He showed up at your church? If that happened, and you didn't recognize Jesus' presence, you would at least take some comfort in knowing that others had made the same mistake. Believe it or not, in our passage today, two of Jesus' very own followers didn't even realize that He was walking with them. While the two men were talking about the things which had happened in the previous days (specifically, the crucifixion of Jesus), Jesus Himself approached them. Rather than recognizing Him for who He was, they simply walked and talked with Him. It wasn't until the end of the journey after He had taught them more of the Word of God and broke bread with them that they realized the Son of God had been in their presence all along.

Did you know that Jesus is in your midst right now? Live like it!

friday Luke 24:28-40

Digging Deeper • How would you respond if Jesus showed up in your living room? Would you ask Him a question you've always wanted to know the answer to, or would you simply freak out? The disciples responded as if they had seen a ghost when Jesus showed up in their midst. They weren't expecting Him at all, especially during the middle of one of their conversations about Him. Jesus comes out of nowhere to minister to and spend time with them. His presence so changed their lives that they returned with great joy. We may not see Jesus, but He is still in our lives. His death and resurrection gave us life-changing salvation, and His example (through the power of the Holy Spirit) changes our behavior.
Take time to think about how the life and death of Christ affects your life today. How are you changed because of Him?

saturday Luke 24:41-53

Digging Deeper • God has given you a homework assignment. Do you know what it is? It's found in all of the gospels, and even the book of Acts. Still can't figure it out? It's known as "The Great Commission" (vv. 46-49). This assignment involves an important task, the one of making disciples. We are to be in the business of leading people to Christ, helping them to grow in their faith, and encouraging them to make more disciples. Just as someone told you about Christ, you should be responsible for telling someone else about Him.
Are you doing your part in fulfilling the Great Commission? Are you doing all you can to make disciples? What could you do differently today?

Week 29

Have you ever had a weird dream? Did you wake up wondering why you dreamed it? Dreams often do not make sense. However, as we look at Ezekiel this week, we will read about visions God gave to him. These visions and signs have a purpose. Pay attention to find out what God is revealing.

prayer focus for this week

the Question — What is the writer saying?

the Answer — How can I apply this to my life?

sunday — Ezekiel 1:1-14

Q

A

Digging Deeper • Ezekiel must have thought it was just another ordinary day. He had no idea that God would take him from being a priest and turn him into a prophet! He was thirty years old when God first spoke to him in a heavenly vision, which was the age when he would take on his role of priestly service. Instead, Ezekiel received a vision from the Lord. A stormy cloud came, and he saw four living creatures. These beings were cherubim. Each had two faces, one human face and one of an animal. This vision had to do with God's judgment on His sinful people.

Are you just going about another ordinary day today? Remember, God has plans for us each and every day. Ask Him to give you an opportunity to make a difference in someone's life today.

monday   Ezekiel 1:15-28

Digging Deeper • Have you ever had a great idea, but when you tried to explain it, no one could understand what you were talking about? Here Ezekiel continues to describe what he saw in the heavenly vision. He gives a great picture of the four living creatures and the wheel, which followed them. He then describes the throne of God. Can you imagine seeing this throne? No matter how well it is described, we cannot comprehend the majesty until we see it ourselves. When Ezekiel saw this scene, he knew he was seeing the likeness of the glory of God and fell on his face. **Ezekiel experienced a glimpse of the glory of the Lord (v. 28). What a powerful thing! How did Ezekiel respond? How should we respond to our awesome and holy God today?**

tuesday   Ezekiel 2:1 - 3:7

Digging Deeper • Have you ever felt God call you to speak to someone about Him? Have you had a desire to witness to a friend or stranger? It can be scary. You may have a fear of rejection or ridicule. What will they think? This passage is the call of God to Ezekiel, where He speaks to Ezekiel and makes him a prophet. The Lord tells him that he is to go to rebellious Israel. He is not to be afraid, but to know that he will be ignored because the people of Israel have also been ignoring the Lord. God will give him the words to speak to His rebellious people. Even if they ignore him, they will at least know a prophet has been among them. **Have you been too afraid to witness to someone? Too scared to do something you know God has called you to do? Pray and ask Him for help. He will give you the courage and the words.**

wednesday Ezekiel 3:8-23

Digging Deeper • After the vision, the Lord returns Ezekiel to his fellow citizens. For seven days Ezekiel sits distressed, most likely because of the burden of the hard assignment the Lord has given him. After seven days, God comes and speaks to him, calling him to be a watchman over Israel. He tells Ezekiel what he is to say and gives him his duties. He is responsible to warn people of the impending judgment if they do not turn from their wicked ways. Ezekiel had an obligation before the Lord, to warn the people, and God would give him the words. Likewise, we have an obligation to share the good news of God's salvation to others.

What about you? Have you been stubborn against what God wants you to do? Have you turned away like the Israelites and rebelled against your Savior? Today is the day to repent and get right with the Lord.

thursday Ezekiel 8:1-6, 16-18

Digging Deeper • What consumes your thoughts or your time, especially when you wake up in the morning? These things may be good things, but they can easily become idols. In this passage, the Lord appears to Ezekiel again. This time he gives him a vision of the judgment upon those who commit idolatry. Ezekiel sees four visions, each one with the Israelites showing greater idolatry. This idolatry is provoking God to jealousy because it is taking the place of the worship that God alone deserves. The scene of verses 16-18 in the inner court of the temple shows one of the holiest areas of worship. The men are worshiping the sun rather than God.

What is it in your life that comes before your relationship with God? It's time to put that idol back in its rightful spot.

friday   Ezekiel 10:1-5, 18-22

Digging Deeper • Do you ever find yourself in awe of the glory of God? The creatures in this passage are the same cherubim as described in chapter one. The man in white linen is an angel chosen to bring judgments on Jerusalem. The coals the man scattered represent judgment being poured out upon Israel for their rebellion against the Lord. Even though God administers judgment upon Israel, it is still His ultimate goal that there be restoration. In verses 18-22, we see the cherubim, symbolizing the glory of the Lord, leave the temple and move to the east gate because God's glory cannot dwell in the temple with the sin of the Israelites.

Have you been taking the things of God lightly? Is there sin in your life that is hindering your fellowship with God and other believers? If so, take care of it today.

saturday   Ezekiel 11:14-25

Digging Deeper • Have you ever moved to a different city or state? It takes a while to make the new place feel like home. Many of the Israelites had been taken captive to Babylon. They felt that they had been forgotten. In verse 13 Ezekiel asks the Lord if He will completely destroy the remnant of Israel. God tells him that although the people of Israel may be exiled in Babylon, He is still a sanctuary for them in that foreign land. God tells Ezekiel that He will gather them together again and give them an undivided heart and a new spirit. This will happen in the Messianic Age.

What about you? Is your heart divided between the things of God and the things of this world? What can you do to change that today? How has God promised to help you?

This week we'll be reading God's instructions to Ezekiel, the words of prophecy God wanted Ezekiel to speak to Israel. Pay close attention as we see the results of the Israelites' sin, God's patience and love for them, and His call for them to repent.

prayer focus for this week

the Question the Answer

What is the writer saying?

How can I apply this to my life?

sunday Ezekiel 12:17-28

Digging Deeper • Do you spend a lot of time worrying about things that are going to happen years from now? Probably not. We usually worry about things that could happen in the near future. In this passage the Lord gives instructions to Ezekiel that are to serve as a warning to the people of the nearness of God's judgment upon Jerusalem and the land of Judah. Ezekiel is to eat and drink with trembling and anxiety to show them God's judgments would no longer delay, since the people did not take God's prophets seriously and were not worried by prophecies.

Are you concerned about the consequences of sin in your life? Or do you think that you can worry about it later? God wants us to have a right relationship with Him *today*. What can you do to make your heart right with God?

monday Ezekiel 13:1-9, 20-23

Digging Deeper • Have you ever heard someone speak about God's Word, and you knew what they were saying was not true? In today's passage the Lord tells Ezekiel to warn the false prophets and prophetesses. They have been speaking falsehood and lying about visions. The false prophets were promising peace when God was saying destruction would come. They were giving the people false comfort by telling them what they wanted to hear. The prophetesses were dabbling with magic. God would not tolerate them misleading His people any longer.

If someone is saying he is speaking for the Lord, but it doesn't match up with Scripture, it is wrong. The best way to avoid false teaching is by knowing the truth, being in the Word of God.

tuesday Ezekiel 14:1-11

Digging Deeper • Are you serving God outwardly while inwardly holding on to activities and making choices that do not honor Him? Notice here how the elders had taken the idols into their heart. They were not just dabbling in idolatry, but were committed to it. God tells Ezekiel to tell the men to repent and turn way from the idols. He wanted them to return to Him. He wanted to be their God. If they continued in their sin, they would be judged.

Often, sin starts with us dabbling in something we don't think is dangerous but eventually becomes more important than God in our lives. What things have you let become more important than God? How can you give your worship to God instead? What habits can you change today to make sure other idols don't show up in your life?

wednesday   Ezekiel 14:12-23

Digging Deeper • Can you remember times you've disobeyed your parents and been punished? Or broken a rule at school and been disciplined by a teacher? There are consequences for our wrong actions. The Lord describes four judgments that He is bringing against Jerusalem: famine, wild beasts, sword, and plague. Even the presence of three righteous men—Noah, Daniel, and Job—would not delay the judgments on the nation's rebellion. But verse 22 says that there will be a remnant that will survive the destruction. And in verse 23 the Lord promises that these things will not happen without cause.

We may not understand it, but God's judgment is always righteous. People bring His judgment when they disobey His clear commands. How can you make sure you are obeying God today?

thursday   Ezekiel 18:1-18

Digging Deeper • Have you ever tried to blame someone else for something you did? Or perhaps you were the one who got blamed? The Jews had come to a point where they were blaming their ancestors' sin for their current problems. They even used a popular proverb to support their thoughts (v. 2). God says that this won't be quoted anymore, for each individual is responsible for his own sin. The same is true today. We are not considered okay by God because our parents or friends are living well, just as we are not condemned by God because of the sin other people we know commit. We answer to the Lord only for ourselves.

When you stand before God, you will give an account of your sin. Is there anything that you've been doing that you know is wrong, but you excuse it?

friday   Ezekiel 18:19-32

Digging Deeper • Have you ever directly disobeyed someone? You may have known what was right, but you chose to do the opposite. God's asking for our obedience is rooted in His love for us. In this second half of chapter 18, He begs Israel to repent and turn from their ways because their iniquity will bring them to ruin, and He does not want them to suffer. He does not find pleasure in their death but wants them to turn back to Him and live by changing their attitude toward Him, and Him changing them (v. 31—"a new heart and a new spirit"). God loves us just as much and wants us to do the same.

How does your attitude toward sin change when you know that God is asking for your obedience because He loves you? What sin can you turn away from today to show your love for Him?

saturday   Ezekiel 20:1-16

Digging Deeper • Do you feel upset or loved when you are disciplined? The Lord disciplines us because of His love for us. God promised blessings in delivering His people from Egypt and leading them into the Promised Land, but they rebelled and disobeyed, worshiping idols and complaining. They had to wander in the wilderness for forty years. An entire generation missed the blessing God had planned for them! All along, God kept withholding His judgment and asking them to return to Him and to the blessings He had for them.

God has great things planned for your life. But have you been too busy doing your own thing? Take time to ask God what He desires of you. You'll find out that His plans for you are better than your own!

This week will focus on the Lord's punishment of Israel for its disobedience. He wants the people of Israel to turn from their ways, and they refuse. They think living in sin is more pleasurable—but the pleasures of sin are only for a short time. We can learn a great lesson from their story—not to follow their footsteps!

prayer focus for this week

the Question — What is the writer saying?

the Answer — How can I apply this to my life?

sunday — Ezekiel 20:17-32

Q

A

Digging Deeper • Do you listen to instruction, or do you do what you want? In today's passage, we see that the next generation continued in their rebellion against God's laws, even after seeing the results of their ancestors' sin. Ezekiel is to speak to the people about their rejection of God. God commands them not to repeat the mistakes of their forefathers by continuing to ignore Him. They should have seen the results of such behavior. God is calling them not to repeat it.

What examples can you think of where people who have gone before you have showed you how *not* to live? How does this affect your decisions? God places people in our lives as examples. Let's learn from the sin of others and not fall into it ourselves.

monday   Ezekiel 20:33-44

Digging Deeper • Do you take time to remember all that God has done for you? In verse 34 we read about not only releasing the exiles out of Babylon but also the future re-gathering of Israel. In verse 39 the Lord tells the people to go to their idols. This may seem out of character since He has been telling the people to avoid idols and return to Him. However, God does not force us to love and serve Him. He wants that to be our desire. If the Israelites refused to listen to the Lord, He would allow them to continue on in sin. But if they turn back to Him, He would accept His people back and show His holiness to them. His purpose in judgment is restoration. **God's desire is always that we would be restored to complete fellowship with Him. If there is something in the way, it's time to get rid of it.**

tuesday   Ezekiel 22:1-4, 23-31

Digging Deeper • Have you ever made a promise to God? Did you keep that promise? The people of Israel had promised obedience to God but turned from Him. They were guilty of shedding blood and being defiled by idolatry. In the Old Testament, until Christ's death and resurrection, the law God had given them to live by was the Mosaic Law (found in Leviticus 17-26). God's people had broken every guideline, and He was angry. He had given them clear instructions for happy and righteous living, and in turn they had rejected it to live according to their feelings and to dwell in their sin. **Do you sometimes think living the Christian life is hard? It shouldn't be. God gives us commands not to restrain us but to warn us and set us free.**

wednesday Ezekiel 26:1-14

Digging Deeper • Have you ever been secretly happy when you saw someone else get punished for their sin? As sinful humans, it is easy to find pleasure when someone who we feel deserves judgment gets it. However, that is not our place. When the city of Tyre sees the judgment brought on Jerusalem, it rejoiced. The people of Tyre thought that the destruction of Jerusalem would profit them because they would gain all the business that Jerusalem would have had. But God would not tolerate their happiness over Jerusalem's destruction. God, now speaking through Ezekiel once again, says this time Tyre will be punished, in the same way that Jerusalem was. She will have enemies come against her and will be torn down. **Have you ever been happy when others suffer for their sin? How can you make sure your life is not calling for the judgment of God?**

thursday Ezekiel 28:11-17

Digging Deeper • Have you ever boasted about what you've accomplished? Have there been times when you let the sin of pride infect your life? Today we see that the king of Tyre thought he was as wise as a god. He had fallen captive to the same lie as Satan, thinking he could be as great as the Most High God. Satan used the prince and king of Tyre to accomplish his purpose. This king was caught up in his own accomplishments and beauty. He allowed what could be used for God's glory to instead fuel his own ego and agenda. But God would put an end to this. These verses are a lament over the death of this king, for his life was wasted. **The king of Tyre had the sin of pride. It brought him to the point where he thought of himself as a god! Anytime we think we know better than God and go our own way, we are guilty of the same sin.**

f**r**id**a**y   Ezekiel 33:1-9

Digging Deeper • Does your school have bells that ring to signal the beginning or end of class—telling you where you should be? Well, during this time in history, when a city was attacked, there was a designated watchman. He would warn the city of enemies approaching by blowing a trumpet to signify danger. If the watchman did his job, then everyone would be warned, but each individual was responsible to hear the call and protect himself. Ezekiel was designated as a watchman for Israel, but not against physical attacks. He was to tell the people that God would destroy them if they did not repent of their idolatry.

We can also be watchmen today for those who have not heard the good news of salvation. Who can you warn about the judgment that will come if people do not turn to God and repent of their sins?

s**a**tu**r**d**a**y   Ezekiel 33:10-20

Digging Deeper • Do you ever try to tell God what is best for you, or think that His ways are not just or right? Those thoughts stem out of our sinful desire to live as we please. God tells Ezekiel that He doesn't want the people to be destroyed. He is giving them this warning because His desire is that they repent and turn from their sin. Israel is beginning to see that it is their sin that has brought them to this point, yet the people are not ready to give up living in their own sinful ways. God is extending them an opportunity to turn, and He won't count their sin against them...yet, they still refuse to do what they know is right.

There is a difference between regretting something and actually repenting of it. Is there something in your life you've been feeling bad about but are not truly repentant over? It's time for us to start hating sin.

Have you ever gotten something you didn't deserve? Maybe it was a good grade on a project that you didn't put much effort into or an unexpected gift. As we further study Ezekiel this week, we will see the amazing forgiveness and love God demonstrates towards Israel. It's completely undeserved!

prayer focus for this week

the Question What is the writer saying?

the Answer How can I apply this to my life?

sunday Ezekiel 33:21-33

Digging Deeper • Has there ever been a time in your life when you received a shocking piece of news? In today's passage, Ezekiel gets information that will change his life. He hears word from a refugee who had escaped that the city of Jerusalem had fallen. You would think that a catastrophic event like that would bring the people of Israel to their knees, but even after God opens Ezekiel's mouth to speak, the people still did not repent. They thought, even in their disobedience, that they had rights to possess the land.

When have you suffered a consequence for your sin? Did it bring you to a point of repentance, or did you just blame God? Can you go back through those times and thank God for the times He has corrected you (Hebrews 12:5-7)—acknowledging that it was for your good?

monday Ezekiel 34:1-16

Digging Deeper • Think of an example of someone in leadership in your life. What kind of role model are they? We all have seen examples of both good and bad leadership, and today's passage gives us another example of the bad kind. Ezekiel's new message is to the "shepherds of Israel." This term refers to the political leaders and kings of this time. The Lord rebukes them through Ezekiel. It was their responsibility to care for their sheep—God's people. Yet they were brutal and harsh to them. They didn't really care for those they ruled. Instead, they had a long list of accusations against them! Now the Lord will take leadership over the nation and provide for them.

Are you a good leader? Do you seek what is best for your relationship with others? Or are you looking out for your own best interests?

tuesday Ezekiel 34:17-31

Digging Deeper • Do you ever have a hard time liking someone who has wronged you? It's hard to care for people who are not caring; however, God is not like that. Here we see that God plans to put a stop to this injustice against His people. Despite their sin, His love for them does not change. The shepherd of verse 23 is a reference to David, whom God will use to reconfirm the Davidic Covenant, which blesses Israel. In verse 25, we see a promise of a covenant of peace. Under the Mosaic Law, blessings were a result of obedience. Now, the Lord will choose to bless His people despite their unfaithfulness.

It is amazing to think about the patience, love, and forgiveness of God. How does your attitude toward God and doing right reflect your always-loving God? Are there areas where you need to be more thankful?

wednesday   Ezekiel 36:1-15

Digging Deeper • Do you ever feel like you're alone in something you really care about? Do you feel you are at the end of your rope? Israel had recently been defeated and taken over by other nations. But now God would punish those who had slandered and damaged Israel. There would be renewed abundance in Israel, shown by the people being able to plant food and eat from their own land again. The population would increase, and the nation would be rebuilt, becoming more prosperous than before. All this speaks of a time still in the future, when Israel will be united again.

We deserve nothing except eternal separation from God, but God still blesses us—and not just with salvation. He also helps us be free from sin's bondage and enjoy earthly blessings. What can you thank God for?

thursday   Ezekiel 36:16-25

Digging Deeper • When people look at you, what do they see? What does your life say to others? In our passage today, God describes the way that Israel had acted towards Him and His commands. The people had lived in an unclean way and been defiled by idol worship, so God poured His wrath on them and scattered them among many nations. They gave God's name a bad example, and people wondered why God's chosen people would act in such a way. So, for the sake of God's holy name, He chose to restore the nation, so that His name would be glorified. He would cleanse the people from their ways and make them a good testimony.

Is your life showing that you know and love God? Can people see a difference in you? What would people say you value and believe? What specific areas of your life can you change to better reflect God?

friday   Ezekiel 36:26-38

Digging Deeper • Have you ever had a wonderful experience of repentance? One where you could definitely sense the comfort of knowing God loves you despite your failures and mistakes? In this passage, God promises to clean and restore His people. He will put a new heart and spirit in them, and they will walk in His ways and obey His commands. They will be clean. God will not do this for their sake, but for His name's sake. He will deliver them and bless them so that people we see will declare that the Lord is God. His holiness cannot tolerate sin. They ought to be ashamed and rejected, but instead God chooses to protect and restore.

We are so much like Israel! We neglect God Who saved us. When is the last time you were truly repentant of your sins? How can you seek God's restoration today?

saturday   Ezekiel 37:1-14

Digging Deeper • Have you ever been in a situation that felt hopeless, like there was no way out? Israel is in that place here. In this passage, the Lord gives a vision where Ezekiel is in the middle of a valley filled with dry bones. God tells Ezekiel to prophesy over the bones, and He will breathe into them so they will regain flesh and live. When Ezekiel obeys the Lord, breath fills the bones, and a great army forms. This vision represents that although Israel is in a lost and hopeless state, they will be restored by the Lord. The nation of Israel will have a revival and be brought back to its Promised Land. By God restoring this lost nation, people will know that God is the Lord. When this day comes, God will receive all the glory!

Is your life a testimony of God's grace? If you know Him as your Savior, you have an obligation to make sure that God receives the honor and glory.

As believers, God is at work in us each and every day. This week we'll see God's treatment of people, both through His faithful justice against those in opposition to His plan and His undeserved blessing on His people.

prayer focus for this week

the Question

the Answer

What is the writer saying?

How can I apply this to my life?

sunday   Ezekiel 37:15-28

Q

A

Digging Deeper • The Lord asks Ezekiel to take two sticks and write on them. One represents Judah, and the other Israel. They will become one in Ezekiel's hand. When the people ask why this is, he is to tell them that the Lord will make Israel and Judah one nation again, referring to a future time when Israel and Judah will be reunited. They will have one King and will be obedient to the Lord. God will make an everlasting covenant with them, and they will flourish in their land as He dwells among them.

What a beautiful phrase in verse 27: "I will be their God, and they shall be my people." God loves Israel despite her disobedience. God also loves you, despite your sin. How can you thank God for His faithfulness today? What unconfessed sin can you deal with now?

monday   Ezekiel 38:1-12

Digging Deeper • Here the Lord tells Ezekiel to prophesy against the chief prince of Meshech and Tubal. In the future, the city of Gog will start a battle against Israel. This passage is a prophecy that their endeavor will fail. God's plan is for them to not only be destroyed, but even be eaten up by wild animals after they die! God takes any attacks on His people seriously. The evil schemes of these people will not prevail. In this seemingly impossible situation for Israel, the Lord will demonstrate His holiness in that this nation's almost sure victory will end in defeat.

What a blessing, as Christians, to be children of God. We know that He loves us and is watching out for us. We have protection in Him that is greater than what anyone else could ever give!

tuesday   Ezekiel 38:13-23

Digging Deeper • Have you ever had an experience in your life that you knew was the hand of God? Sometimes you can see it in a person or situation that only He could change. In this passage God's holiness will be displayed right before His people. They will witness God's protection on their behalf. The anger of the Lord will well up against Gog and be shown through torrential rain, hailstones, burning sulfur, and plague. All of these disasters are elements of nature that only God controls. Through these judgments, God will make Himself known.

Think of the amazing ways God has gone before you and protected you in your life. Sometimes we think that what happens in life is by chance. How can you change your attitude toward life to see everything as under the control of God? What can you praise Him for?

wednesday Ezekiel 39:1-16

Digging Deeper • Can you think of a time when you saw pictures or a video of destruction from a war? This passage is a further description of the destruction the Lord will bring upon Gog for trying to defeat Israel. Israel will be able to make fires for seven years with the amount of weaponry that will be left after the destruction of the army of Gog. It will take seven months to bury all the people of Gog. This destruction comes from God keeping His Word when it comes to judgment. He won't let His name be abused anymore. All the nations will see God at work.

God takes sin seriously and He is a protector of His people. Even if we don't see those opposed to God being punished today, we can trust that God will be just. Do you struggle with feeling like unrighteous people don't get punished for their wrong? How can these verses help you today?

thursday Ezekiel 39:17-29

Digging Deeper • Have you ever felt compassion for someone going through a hard time? The Lord has compassion on His people by being their protector and provider, just as He was for their ancestors. In a continuation from yesterday's passage, we read today about the cleanup process after the people of Gog are destroyed. The Israelites give a proper burial for their enemies; however, they will not be able to bury them fast enough, and birds will eat many of the corpses. This future act will be a testimony not only to them but also to the surrounding nations of God's greatness.

God demonstrates His compassion to us each and every day. How can you show God's compassion to those around you today—especially those who may have wronged you before?

friday   Ezekiel 43:1-9; 44:1-4

Digging Deeper • When was the last time you had a wonderful time in God's Word? Could you sense God teaching and guiding you? Imagine actually seeing the glory of God! In this vision from the Lord, Ezekiel is taken into the inner court, which is filled with the glory of the Lord. When Ezekiel sees this glory, he falls flat on his face. God wanted Ezekiel to communicate His holiness so the people would come to repentance. When we see even a glimpse of God and Who He is, it should bring into perspective how sinful we are and how desperately we need a Savior!

As sinful humans, we often try to be in control of our circumstances. What situation will you turn over to the Lord today?

saturday   Ezekiel 47:1-12

Digging Deeper • What is the most beautiful place you can think of? Maybe somewhere you've been on vacation, or a special place you've discovered? This passage continues telling about Ezekiel's vision from the Lord. God brings Ezekiel around to the front of the temple, where water is flowing from the south side. Each time the water is measured, it is deeper, representing blessing. The river eventually flows to the Red Sea, giving new life to a dry, forsaken place. On the banks of the river there is an abundance of trees, very similar to the fertile land of the Garden of Eden. God is blessing in more ways than one can imagine, and it's only the beginning of what is to come!

Isn't God's creation wonderful? God truly has created a beautiful world. The scene described here is beyond the most beautiful places we have seen. Why not thank God today for what He has created and the beautiful things we have yet to see in Heaven?

Week 34.

Which is easier to read: a letter from someone who is mad at you, or a letter from a good friend who wants to give you some practical advice? As Paul writes to his companions in Philippi, you can sense the love between them. This week you, too, will get some very practical advice from our *good friend*, the Apostle Paul. Read on!

prayer focus for this week

the Question — What is the writer saying?

the Answer — How can I apply this to my life?

sunday Philippians 1:1-7

Q

A

Digging Deeper • "I thought you said you were finished cleaning your room," your mom says as she looks through your bedroom door. "I *am* finished," you reply. She shakes her head: "Finished? You call this clean?" Sometimes getting a job done is difficult, and we give up halfway through. What if God decided not to finish the work He began in you? What if He decided that He had kept you saved long enough and He was tired of it? It is great to know that that will not happen. The Apostle Paul and Timothy, as they wrote to the Christians at Philippi, reminded them that God was going to finish the work that He began in them (v. 6). They could be confident that God would not give up halfway through—He would finish the job.

How can God's faithfulness encourage you to live a confident Christian life? Having this confidence, how will you be bold for Christ this week?

monday Philippians 1:8-14

Digging Deeper • It's scary to think how your life can influence others. Evidently, some of the difficulties that the Apostle Paul had faced were reported to the people of Philippi. Paul reminds them that God can be glorified and others can be impacted through hard times. Paul says that the difficulties he faced happened so that the Gospel could be shared in many different places (v. 12). In fact, he says that because of his bonds (being in jail), Christ was preached in several places, including the palace. Another result of Paul's hardships was the influence these situations had on others. Because Paul was thrown into prison, other Christians were "much more bold to speak the Word without fear" due to his influence (v. 14).

How does your life influence others? How can you help others be "more bold" to preach the Gospel?

tuesday Philippians 1:15-21

Digging Deeper • What is your passion? Fill in the blank: It doesn't matter what happens, as long as I get to … *what?* The Apostle Paul was all about Jesus Christ being lifted up, and about being able to preach the Word of God. He says that different people preach Jesus Christ in different ways. Paul does not worry about the method. He is excited that Jesus Christ is being preached (vv. 15-18). He says that his driving passion (v. 20: "earnest expectation and my hope") is that Christ is glorified, whether Paul lives or dies. To Paul, life is Christ and death is gain (v.. 21). Paul's passion was Jesus Christ and Him glorified. Again, what is your passion?

Will you make Jesus Christ your passion? How can Christ be the center of your life today?

wednesday Philippians 1:22-30

Digging Deeper • Who is your biggest encourager? Who is the person who helps you become a better person? For the people of Philippi, it was Paul. He wanted to go to Heaven, but he knew these people needed him to be with them to build up their morale (vv. 23-24). But Paul also encouraged them to live a godly life even if he was not around (v. 27). It would have been easy to live godly while he was present, but he wanted their lifestyle to go beyond what they felt they *had to* do to something they *wanted to*. Even if he was not with them, he wanted to be able to hear reports of godly living and unity, and for them to stand on their own two feet spiritually, because he knew they would soon face suffering (v. 29).

Who is an encouragement in your life? How does that person point you to Christ, and how can you be an encouragement to someone today?

thursday Philippians 2:1-8

Digging Deeper • Have you ever heard the phrase, "Like father, like son"? It means that a father and son act alike or think alike because they are related. If you are a Christian, you are now *related* to Jesus Christ, and your actions should reveal this. Paul says, "Let this mind (attitude) be in you, which was also in Christ Jesus" (v. 5). This entire passage hinges on this verse. If you have the mind of Christ, you will be unified with other believers (v. 2), you will think of others before yourself (vv. 3-4), you will not be puffed up (v. 7), you will be a servant (v. 7), and be humble and obedient (v. 8). If you are a Christian, act like a Christian (Christ-like). Begin by having the mind of Christ.

How can you have the mind of Christ? What will you do today that will make you think and act more like Christ?

friday Philippians 2:9-16

Digging Deeper • What's in a name? Well, "at the name of Jesus every knee should bow … every tongue should confess that Jesus Christ is Lord" (v. 10). The name of Jesus is a precious name. In verse 12, when Paul says, "wherefore," he means that because this statement is true (that all will bow), we should "work out [our] own salvation with fear and trembling." Work out our salvation? What does that mean? Since Jesus is Who He is and has saved us from our sin, we should work for Him. We are not working to obtain salvation but working because we have received it. While we are working, we must remember not to complain or murmur (v. 14) so we might shine as lights as we "hold forth the word of life" (vv. 15-16).

What work (Christian Service) can you do today? How will that work give honor and glory to the name of Jesus Christ?

saturday Philippians 2:17-23

Digging Deeper • What kind of reputation do you have? In yesterday's passage, we learned that we were to *work* because we have been saved. Do others know that you work for Jesus Christ? When your name is mentioned, do you have the reputation of one who serves God? Paul decided that Timothy was going to make a trip to visit the people of Philippi. As he discussed the young Timothy in his letter, he drew attention to the reputation that Timothy already had with the church. Paul said, "Ye know the proof of him…he hath served with me in the gospel" (v. 22). The church at Philippi knew that Timothy was a godly man.

What do people think when your name is mentioned? How can you improve how you show Christ? What kind of things does a godly person do?

Paul wrapped up his letter to his friends in Philippi with more practical advice. He wanted the members of this church to live successful Christian lives. To gain wisdom on how to be unselfish, humble, focused, secure, and giving—and to have a godly thought life—read and apply the message of this week's passages.

prayer focus for this week

the Question What is the writer saying?

the Answer How can I apply this to my life?

sunday   Philippians 2:24-30

Q

A

Digging Deeper • Who is the most unselfish person you know? Paul had a good friend and fellow worker named Epaphroditus. Paul said that this guy not only ministered to him in the things that were necessary, but also in the things that Paul wanted (v. 25). Paul reported to the church at Philippi that Epaphroditus had been sick—so sick he was about to die. However, God had mercy on him and healed him. Paul told the church that Epaphroditus had become sick while doing God's work. This guy was so unselfish he almost died ministering to the needs and wants of Paul because the church at Philippi was unable to help him due to the distance (v. 30). What do you do to help your church grow? How can you use your life to fill the needs or the goals of those around you? How can you be more unselfish for the cause of Christ?

Sometimes I rely on my appearance

monday **Philippians 3:1-6**

Q

Unconditional Love
Merciful and Gracious
Justified by faith
Cast Anxieties on Him

A *Sometimes don't make sense but has made the human Being that I am, give purpose in life.*

Digging Deeper • Do you know people who think they are really great or important? Doesn't it make you sick? Paul reminds us that if we ever get to the point where we start bragging about how good we are, we need to think again. Paul had a pretty good religious background (vv. 5-6), but that was not what made him a good Christian. He says that true Christians "worship God in the spirit…rejoice in Christ Jesus, and have no confidence in the flesh" (v. 3). Our abilities and heritage should not be the center of attention. We must worship the Lord in the spirit, and our rejoicing must be in Jesus Christ, not in our accomplishments.

Do you rely on what you've done—even good things—for confidence? Name some things that Christ has done in you that are more important than earthly things. What can you do to *decrease* so that Christ can *increase*?

tuesday **Philippians 3:7-14**

Digging Deeper • What goals do you have for your life? What needs to happen in order for you to achieve them? If you are going to reach any of your goals, you must stay focused. In this passage, Paul is the epitome of focus. He considers any accomplishment and every ambition to be worthless compared to knowing Christ (v. 8). He wants to know Christ in His resurrection, in His suffering, and in His death (v. 10). Paul considers himself and his past accomplishments unimportant and stays focused on the prize of the "high calling of God in Christ Jesus" (v. 14).

What do you usually focus on (think about) throughout the day? Has anything taken your focus off Christ? How will you make Jesus Christ the most important person in your life today?

wednesday   Philippians 3:15-21

Digging Deeper • Did you ever play follow-the-leader when you were younger? What you did and where you went depended on the type of leader you had. Paul tells the people of Philippi to follow his example. He encourages them to have the same mind set as he had when it came to forgetting the past and pressing on to the future (vv. 15-16). However, Paul does not act like he is the only one doing right. He tells them to "mark" (note) others who live righteously as examples to follow as well. He warns us to stay away from those who walk like the world because our citizenship is not of this world, but of Heaven (vv. 18-20).

Have you been following the example or the advice of ungodly people in any area of your life? If so, what can you do to change your habits and seek out godly influences instead? How will you follow Christ this week?

thursday   Philippians 4:1-7

Digging Deeper • Do you ever feel insecure? It is an uneasy feeling. Without security and structure, anyone would begin to worry. If the world is crashing down, how can anyone not worry? Paul gives some practical advice in the form of a command: "Be careful [anxious] for nothing" (v. 6). In essence, Paul says, "Stop worrying about things." Easier said than done, right? Well, Paul knew that, so he gave us a way to stop worrying. Instead of worrying, we should pray, making our requests known to God. The result? We get peace, but not just any peace. We get the peace of God. A peace that Paul says "shall keep (guard) your hearts and minds" (v. 7). The word *keep* literally means "to fortify." Talk about security!

Do you want peace and security in your life? In what situation do you need to stop worrying and begin trusting and praying?

friday Philippians 4:8-13

Digging Deeper • Whatever you do, do not think about a "Big Mac"! "Big Macs" are sold at McDonalds. Do not think about a "Big Mac"! Listen! Stop thinking about a "Big Mac"! What is the easiest way to stop thinking about a "Big Mac"? That's right, think about something else! We should not be thinking about evil things. So Paul gives us eight replacement thoughts (v. 8). To think only on things that are true, honest, just, pure, lovely, of good report, virtuous, and praiseworthy is tough in today's society. But Paul reminds the church to follow his example (v. 9), both in thinking on good things and also for learning how to be content in everyday life. He reminds us that, through Christ, we can do both.
What do you think about that should be replaced with the thoughts of Christ? In what circumstances do you need to be content?

saturday Philippians 4:14-23

Digging Deeper • The Apostle Paul finishes his letter to the church at Philippi with praise. He notes how generous they have been in providing for his financial needs. When he first began doing missionary work, they were the only support he had (v. 15). While he was in Thessalonica, the Philippian believers sent help to him twice (v. 16). Paul made it very clear that he was not interested in getting money but in seeing the Gospel spread around the world. In response to their giving, Paul affirmed the fact that God would in turn supply their need (v. 19). Ultimately, Paul desired that God would receive all the glory (v. 20).
What sacrifices can you make to help support a missionary? Who specifically will you support? Will you consider giving not only money but also yourself?

Picture yourself on a treasure hunt for precious diamonds. You prepare to enter the mine and dig until you find the precious stones. But before you even make it to the mineshaft, you see diamonds all over the ground in front of you. Reading Isaiah is like finding diamonds on the ground; you see Jesus on page after page!

prayer focus for this week

the Question What is the writer saying?

the Answer How can I apply this to my life?

sunday Isaiah 1:1-9, 16-20

Digging Deeper • Isaiah is God's prophet; he is speaking for God. God is pleading with His disobedient children who have rebelled against Him. They are sinful, backslidden, beaten, sick, faint, wounded, bruised, and diseased. Their country is desolate, and unless God spares them, there will be nothing left! The good news starts in verse 16—they can be washed and cleansed, but only one way (v. 18), through the washing of the blood of Christ that is to come (1 Peter 1:18-20)!

Are you living only for yourself? How are you doing? Why not turn to Christ as the source for your cleansing today?

monday Isaiah 4:2-6

Digging Deeper • Isaiah looks right past the dark days of Israel and into the Millennial Kingdom of Christ. The seven years of tribulation have ended, and the earth has been cleansed with judgment and fire. Jesus, as the "Branch of Jehovah," will reign for the thousand years (millennium). It will be a time when Christ will finally be the focus of all human attention and adoration. Even when things look dark and discouraging, we can take comfort in knowing that God has everything under control. Nothing catches Him by surprise.

Can you remember times when God showed His faithfulness to you? How can you draw on these times when your circumstances look dark and discouraging? Why not express your love to Jesus today in prayer?

tuesday Isaiah 5:1-7

Digging Deeper • God loves Israel. He compares her to a beautiful vineyard with everything necessary for beautiful grapes. But what happens? Wild grapes! Now judgment will come as the hedge is torn down and the vineyard gets overrun with weeds, drought, and neglect. The play on words in verse 7 could be translated: "He looked for equity, but got iniquity; for right, but received riot." Six woes are pronounced on Israel from verses 8-22, yet God's hand is stretched out still to forgive in verse 25.

How are you responding to the goodness of God? Have you taken time to praise Him today for His blessings? Why not list your praises in your prayer journal?

wednesday   Isaiah 6:1-13

Digging Deeper • Take off your shoes, you are on holy ground! This is Isaiah's meeting with God and his call into the ministry. Isaiah's King, Uzziah, died as a leper, and Isaiah found himself in the temple. There he encountered Holy God. Isaiah called Him "Adonai," or Master, in verse 1, but by verse 3, he is calling Him "Yahweh," or Jehovah. John 12:41 identifies this Lord Who Isaiah saw that day as Jesus Himself! One of God's primary attributes is holiness, which is mentioned three times in a row (v. 3) to illustrate the Trinity. Seeing God clearly causes Isaiah to say "woe is me." The vision continues with "lo," when his lips were purged of sin, and "go," when God gave him a ministry.
God has a special call for you, just as He had for Isaiah. To find it, follow Isaiah's steps from "woe" to "lo" to "go" and see what God can do!

thursday   Isaiah 7:10-16

Digging Deeper • Have you ever met a mocker? They are the type who say, "Prove it." God tells Isaiah to meet Ahaz, the sinful King of Israel, and warn him of his sinful alliance with the wicked Assyrians. God offers to perform a miraculous sign for Ahaz, but Ahaz refuses the sign. So, bypassing his unbelief, Isaiah tells the whole house of David (and us too) of the miraculous virgin birth to come. Isaiah 7:14 is one of the key verses in the Old Testament that tells us of the virgin birth that brought us our Savior, Jesus Christ. He is Immanuel, God with us! Yes, God proved the point—by sending the Savior through the virgin womb of Mary!
Do you know Jesus Christ as your personal Savior? Why not invite Him into your heart right now? If you know Him, tell someone about Him today!

friday　Isaiah 8:5-18

Digging Deeper • Isaiah had two sons by this time (v. 18) and both were for signs against sinful Israel. Isaiah 7:3 mentions his first son, whose name means "only a remnant shall return (if you disobey)." His second son's name (8:3) means "swift is the treasure, speedy is the prey." Both names are a rebuke to a nation that is in rebellion against God. The nation's judgment comes within two years as Israel is defeated and overrun with Assyrian soldiers (v. 8). Unfortunately, the Immanuel of verse 8, who is the "God with us" of verse 10, is judging, not blessing, them.

Go to the Lord of Hosts, the stone of stumbling (vv. 13-14; 1 Peter 2:8), as your refuge, rather than living a life that will bring His judgment. Do you see Jesus Christ revealed more and more as we press further into Isaiah? Jesus said that these verses were about Himself (Luke 24:27, 44-45).

saturday　Isaiah 8:19 — 9:7

Digging Deeper • How sad to look for God through wizards and satanic spirits. Our living God can be found in the pages of Scripture (8:20)! We have seen Him as the branch of Jehovah (4:2), the virgin-born Immanuel (7:14), and the great light of Galilee (9:2), and now Christ is revealed in 9:6-7 in His full-blown glory as Jehovah! "Child" represents His humanity, "Son" His deity. He is the "Wonderful" (Supernatural) Counselor as He leads, judges, and guides. He is the "mighty God" as a powerful Warrior. He is the "everlasting Father" in that the Messiah is eternally a Father to His people, guarding and supplying their needs.

Isn't Jesus wonderful? Why not praise Him for Who He is today?

Week 37

What is the most exciting trip you have ever been on? Was it to see the Grand Canyon or Niagara Falls? This week we will have an awesome trip through history. From the fall of Satan from Heaven to the ultimate rule of Christ as King of Kings and Lord of Lords, get ready for a great Bible adventure!

prayer focus for this week

the **Question**   What is the writer saying?

the **Answer**   How can I apply this to my life?

sunday   Isaiah 10:16-27

Q

A

Digging Deeper • God proves His unfailing love for Israel in this chapter. The beautiful phrase "For all this His anger is not turned away, but His hand is stretched out still"—found in 5:25; 9:12, 17, 21, and here in 10:4—is illustrated by the story of the Assyrians. God will use the wicked Assyrians to chastise backsliding Israel (v. 6). But God will also destroy the Assyrians, illustrated by the burning down of a forest (vv. 16-19). The Assyrians actually were destroyed just a few years later in Isaiah 37:36, when the death angel killed 185,000 Assyrian soldiers. God makes a further promise to destroy the Assyrians just like he destroyed 135,000 Midianites with Gideon's 300 men (v. 26) in Judges 7:1-26.

Why not take time right now to thank God for His faithfulness and love? Take heart today that God will always have a remnant of faithful followers.

monday   Isaiah 11:1-12

Digging Deeper • Israel and Judah would be chopped down like a stump by Assyria and Babylon. But life will sprout, and it will be Jesus Christ, of the line of David (v. 1). He will be full of the Holy Spirit's power (v. 2). This is a reaffirmation of the covenant God made with David in 2 Samuel 7 and will take place during the Messianic reign of Christ. Christ's reign will be perfect since He is all-knowing, all-wise, and fair (vv. 3-5). All of the animal kingdom will be peaceful (vv. 6-8), and the world will be at rest, filled with the knowledge of God (v. 9). In verses 9-12, God will bring the Jews back from the four corners of the earth (Matthew 24:31).
Thank God today for His precious promises! One day this world, which is so full of war, will be at peace when King Jesus reigns!

tuesday   Isaiah 12:1-6

Digging Deeper • With the kingdom set up, it is time for worship! Don't you love singing the praises of God when you get together with God's people? This short chapter was known as a "Hymn of Praise" by the Jewish teachers. It was chanted at the Feast of Tabernacles as the high priest drew water with a silver pitcher from the Gihon Spring and then poured it on the altar of the temple. It was at this feast, 700 years later, that Jesus called out, "if any man thirst, let him come to me and drink" (John 7:37). At this point many knew that He was the Christ.
Why not sing a song of praise to the Lord right now? Our Lord is our joy, we can sing with joy about our salvation. We have the Holy One of Israel to sing about.

wednesday · Isaiah 13:9-20

Digging Deeper • Isaiah 13-14 predicts the activities of the Babylonians and condemns them. Babylon comes from the city of Babel, which was founded by Nimrod, the first idol worshiper (Genesis 10:9). In Isaiah's time, Babylon was weak, but 100 years later, in 612 B.C., Nineveh, capital of Assyria, fell to the Babylonians. Nebuchadnezzer became king of that empire and attacked Judah. In history and Scripture, Babylon is the center of political and religious rebellion. It has been destroyed once and can be seen in modern Iraq as a desolate place. It will also be destroyed later by Christ in its religious and political rebirth under the Antichrist.

Are you upset by the headlines in the world today? Rest assured that history is HIS story. God is working out His will in the world today and ultimately every knee will bow!

thursday · Isaiah 14:12-17

Digging Deeper • Does he have a pitchfork, horns, a pointed tail, and wear red underwear? Of course you know that Satan is much smarter than the foolish pictures we see so often today. He is an angel of light. He tried to take one of Jesus' own names, "the bright and morning star" (Revelation 22:16—Lucifer means "morning star" or "Venus"). Satan was cast out of Heaven because of his pride. He clearly wants to destroy God and dominate the universe. Look at his five "I wills" in these verses. Verse 15 tells us where he will end up one day.

Do you want God's will or your will? Why not take inventory today of where you are with God. Are you submissive to His will or are you simply living for yourself?

friday Isaiah 24:21 – 25:9

Digging Deeper • Chapters 24-27 are known as the "Little Apocalypse" because it is similar to events predicted in the book of Revelation. Isaiah 24:21-23 is very important because it clearly presents a premillennial time-line sequence: a) Christ returns and punishes the kings, b) He incarcerates them (for 1,000 years according to Revelation 20), and then c) after "many days," they will be punished (at the Great White Throne Judgment of Revelation 20:11). Isaiah 25:1-5 foretells the destruction of Babylon (see also Revelation 17-19), which precedes the blessing of the Millennial Reign of Christ (Isaiah 25:6-12).

Are you ready for the Lord to return today? When He comes, all of these end-time events will unfold. What person do you need to share Christ with today?

saturday Isaiah 26:1-9, 19-21

Digging Deeper • These verses give us a glimpse of the music that we will sing when Christ returns to earth. It will be a day of salvation, truth, and peace. This passage contains one of the great verses of comfort we can use in times of fear (v. 3), and that the Lord Jehovah is our everlasting strength, or literally the "Rock of Ages" (v. 4). Verse 19 reminds us of 1 Thessalonians 4:13-17 and the resurrection at the Rapture. This will lead to a period of judgment in the Tribulation Period that will quickly pass. A time of blessing will follow (vv. 20-21).

Perfect peace comes to those who focus their attention on the Lord. Let's spend today meditating on our wonderful Savior.

Week 38

Have you ever noticed how many different medicines are in your medicine cabinet at home? God opens His medicine cabinet here for sick mankind. The disease is sin, and the cure is provided by our Great Physician through His Word.

prayer focus for this week

the**Question** — **What is the writer saying?**

the**Answer** — **How can I apply this to my life?**

sunday — Isaiah 28:5-15

Digging Deeper • Pride is the downfall of Ephraim (v. 1) just as it was for Satan (Chapter 12). Ephraim will be judged by God, using the Assyrians. One day Christ Himself will be His people's beautiful crown (v. 5), but not until after they fall because of their own pride. Strong warnings are seen against drinking alcohol (vv. 7-8). We also see God's method of teaching doctrine (v. 10). It's simply repetition— "line upon line, precept upon precept, here a little and there a little." Unfortunately, this method of teaching will also be used to teach them why they were to be judged (vv. 13-15).

Do you have a problem with pride or alcohol? Allow God to change your heart by constantly feeding yourself on His Word through quiet time, Bible study, and hearing the preaching of God's Word.

monday Isaiah 28:16-29

Digging Deeper • Ephraim was making promises to the enemy of God, which meant it made a covenant with death and Hell (vv. 15-18). The people should have made a covenant with God (vv. 16-17), their chief cornerstone and master builder, on whose foundation they would never be moved. These verses look forward to Christ, Who is our "Stone." Verses 19-22 describe the judgment of God that would come on His disobedient children. He calls it a "strange work." Verses 23-29 liken God to the "master farmer" who knows just how much effort is needed to harvest different grains. He also knows how to discipline His children.

Have you ever been under the discipline of God for living in disobedience? Our loving Father uses different methods with each of us to get us exactly where we need to be.

tuesday Isaiah 29:13-24

Digging Deeper • God is always interested in our heart's condition, and because He is God, He can see its true state. God's people were being disciplined because of their hypocrisy and ignorance. They said the right words, but their hearts were far from Him. God would again do a "strange act" (28:21) of judgment. The people were confused (vv. 15-16). They didn't realize that God saw everything. He could hide anything from them, but they couldn't hide anything from Him. Still, eventually God will bless the land again (vv. 17-24).

Why not take inventory of your heart condition today? Are you trying to hide anything from God?

wednesday Isaiah 30:8-18

Digging Deeper • In verses 11-12, the Holy One of Israel is mentioned twice. This phrase is used twenty-five times in Isaiah but only thirty-one times in all of Scripture. It tells us that God is separate from everything else in the universe, and therefore, we owe Him honor and obedience. This separateness—being holy—is something that is passed on to us at salvation, when we as saints are set apart to God and become holy, as He is, because of our association with Him. Two pictures are seen of God's judgment on His people: a broken down wall and a broken piece of pottery (vv. 13-14). Once again gracious words of comfort flow from the heart of our loving God (vv. 15-18).

Pray and patiently wait on God to fulfill His perfect will in you, in His time. He will restore you and make you holy if you put your trust in Him.

thursday Isaiah 32:1-4, 13-20

Digging Deeper • When Jesus Christ comes to rule and reign, things will be different (v. 1). His twelve disciples will reign with Him, and we will too. Those who rule will be like Christ, like the shadow of a "Great Rock" (v. 2)! The blind will see, the deaf will hear, and the dumb will speak. Both physical and spiritual healing is indicated here (vv. 3, 14). When Christ reigns (vv. 13-16), what is broken and barren will be changed. The rest of the chapter tells that justice, righteousness, peace, and safety will mark this period for man and beast.

Ask God for quietness and assurance in your heart. Even when all around us is chaos and confusion, Christ offers a hiding place in the shadow of our Great Rock!

friday   Isaiah 33:5-6, 15-22

Digging Deeper • Isaiah now sees the Lord as exalted (vv. 5-6), just as he did in chapter 6 when he was called by God. Now he sees God in His eternal reign, high in Heaven and superior in righteousness. He dispenses judgment and righteousness, wisdom, knowledge, stability, and salvation. Military terms are used to show the safety that comes to the person who is righteous and in the watch-care of the Lord (vv. 18-22). Jesus will govern perfectly as Prophet, Priest, and King (v. 22). **One day we will see the King in His beauty. Until then, let's live like we really do love Jesus. What would you do today if you knew it was your last day to serve Christ on earth?**

saturday   Isaiah 35:1-10

Digging Deeper • Our earth today groans under the weight of sin. Innocent animals die, and humans lie with crippled bodies because of incurable diseases, selfish wars, and sinful actions. But during Christ's reign, what was lost in the fall of man will be regained. Lands lost to sweeping sands will be restored (v. 1). The weak will find strength to live the day without pain (v. 3). All our modern fears will fall before the power of Christ (v. 4). The effects of sin on our health will disappear (vv. 5-6). Best of all, God's holiness will rule this earth (v. 8) and its creatures (v. 9). Imagine being locked in a smelly, dark dungeon for years, then being released into a beautiful utopia. That is what is waiting for God's faithful remnant (v. 10)! **What hardships can you think of today that will be gone when Christ returns?**

The Apostle Peter tells us of "exceeding great and precious promises" that are given to us (2 Peter 1:4). This week's Quiet Time is loaded with such promises. From here to the end of the book we will continue to see Christ in all His glory, and we will learn of new blessings He has in store for those that love Him!

prayer focus for this week

the Question — What is the writer saying?

the Answer — How can I apply this to my life?

sunday — Isaiah 40:1-11

Q

A

Digging Deeper • Starting with Isaiah 40 and going to the end of the book, we will see themes similar to those in the New Testament, such as grace, redemption, the suffering of Christ, salvation, holiness, and the Messianic Kingdom. The first verses of this chapter were used by the famous classical musician, Handel, for his great musical known as "Messiah," which is often sung at Christmas time. Verse 10 announces the coming of the Lord, but the road had to be prepared before the King could come. Elijah and John the Baptist were forerunners of Christ (Malachi 4:5 and Matthew 3:3). The Tribulation will prepare the way for Christ to come a second time and rule in the Millennium.

Are you looking for Christ to return today? The whole earth will exalt Him then; what can you do to praise Him now?

monday Isaiah 40:21-31

Digging Deeper • God calls all of creation to testify to His Lordship. Think about how the wisest men on earth at one point all thought the earth was flat. Even the smartest men are like "grasshoppers" before the mighty God (v. 22). Historical record says that Christopher Columbus knew the world was round because of Isaiah 40:22. But God's greatness is not just something we can look to for guidance; it's also something we can have. God is so great that not only did He also create the billions of stars, but He also named each one (v. 26). He knows the ways of each person (v. 27), and He passes on His great power to us (vv. 29-31) if we wait on Him.

How can you tap into God's greatness today? He promised strength in verse 31—what do you need to do to get it?

tuesday Isaiah 41:8-20

Digging Deeper • God considered Abraham His friend (v. 8), and through this friendship, many people were able to have a relationship with God. The people of the nation of Israel, who this was passage was written to, were some of the people who got to enjoy this friendship and the many blessings that came with it (v. 10). But those of us who have a relationship with God today can also claim the promises in verse 10. Verse 20 tells us the ultimate goal of God's work through Israel, and now us—that the whole world will know this God.

Have you become friends with God? Was your salvation just a transaction, or can you say you know God personally? Look at 2 Corinthians 5:18-20—what can you do to help others become friends with God?

Wednesday Isaiah 42:1-9

Digging Deeper • The King of the universe has a servant—His Son, Jesus Christ. (Notice parallel passages in Matthew 12:17-21 and Philippians 2:5-8.) Verse 1, which talks about God putting His Spirit on Christ, was fulfilled at Christ's baptism. Jesus came as a humble man (vv. 1-4) to fulfill God's covenant with man and be a light to the Gentiles (v. 6). He did this through salvation, where He was fully God (vv. 5-9) and fully man.

Christ is the focus of most Old Testament prophecy, showing that God was thinking about our salvation for many years. Why not thank God for sending Jesus to be our Savior right now?

Thursday Isaiah 43:1-13

Digging Deeper • God loves Israel. He created the people of Israel, named them, owns them, and redeemed them. Ultimately He would provide for their eternal salvation through the death of His "Suffering Servant," seen in Isaiah 53. He brought Israel through water at the Red Sea and Jordan, and He would bring Israel through fire with Shadrach, Meshach, and Abednego. God's restoration would bring earth back to the way it's meant to be—with the blind using their eyes (v. 8), the deaf using their ears (v. 8), and all people believing in Him (v. 10)!

Have you experienced God's awesome love for you by receiving Jesus Christ as your personal Lord and Savior? Can you find another precious promise to claim in these verses?

friday Isaiah 43:14-25

Digging Deeper • When you hear "Thus saith the Lord," you need to listen! Our great and powerful God repeats His names in verse 15 so that we will all pay attention. He will destroy Babylon (v. 14), which will be quenched like the wick of a candle (v. 17). His great rescues of the past (v. 18) won't compare to His rescues in the future. This passage was fulfilled with the rescue from Babylon, which Ezra and Nehemiah recorded, but the ultimate fulfillment of this passage is when all of Israel is gathered during the millennium and the last unsaved Jew is saved. Then, for the first time in Jewish history, "all Israel shall be saved" (Romans 11:26).
The Lord formed Israel (and us) for Himself (v. 21) so that we would praise Him. How does your life praise God today?

saturday Isaiah 44:6-8, 21-24

Digging Deeper • There is only one God, and His name is Jehovah. He is the Lord of Israel. He is the Lord of Hosts ("hosts" refers to the armies of angels that He commands). The prophets are rather sarcastic as they show that all of the other "gods" don't even exist (vv. 6-24). Jehovah claims to be first and last (v. 6)—a claim that God the Father also makes in Revelation 1:8, as does the Son in Revelation 1:11, 17 and 22:13.
We may not have these types of idols today, but we do have plenty of things that people think are worth trusting more than God—people, possessions, money, technology. What things are you foolishly trusting more than God? What will you do to change that today?

Week 40

Is it possible for a teenager today to understand a prophet that lived 2,700 years ago? No way, unless you have God's wisdom! Pray for wisdom today and ask God for an understanding heart. Then watch what happens as you start to understand the inspired words of the amazing Isaiah.

prayer focus for this week

the **Question**   What is the writer saying?

the **Answer**   How can I apply this to my life?

sunday   Isaiah 45:5-13

Q

A

Digging Deeper • God was going to use a Gentile king (Cyrus) to deliver 50,000 people from Babylon (vv. 1-5). When this happened in 539 B.C., a river was diverted from under the wall of Babylon, and King Cyrus' soldiers sneaked underneath. Notice that God predicted this almost 200 years before it happened. Verse 6 shows that God's protection isn't only for Israel—it includes those who are saved in the western world today. God's power is so great that He not only created good but also the judgment (v. 7— "evil") to combat the destruction that comes from man's sin. Verse 13 takes us back to Cyrus and reminds us He even uses unbelievers to do His will.

God works through our evil (v. 7) and unbelieving men (vv. 1-5, 13). How can you see Him working through you, even when you have messed up?

monday   Isaiah 45:14-25

Digging Deeper • Egypt, Ethiopia, and the Sabeans (Queen of Sheba), all currently Muslim areas, will one day come and worship the true God (v. 14). God's ability to do amazing things—such as bring these people to Him—will help the world finally see that He is the only God (v. 14), although He's already told them this many times (vv. 21-23). He may sometimes seem hidden (v. 15), but these verses show that this God of salvation does nothing in vain. One day everyone will bow to Him (v. 23—see Philippians 2:10).

How has God shown you in your life that He is the only God worth serving? How can you trust God today, perhaps in a situation where God's plan seems hidden from you?

tuesday   Isaiah 46:3-13

Digging Deeper • The Babylonians had to carry their idols (vv. 1-2), but God carried the Israelites (vv. 3-4). Verses 5-7 remind us of the foolishness of making an idol and then worshiping the thing; we have already seen how God mocks those who fashion idols and worship them. God declares His exclusivity again in verses 8-10. His argument to "prove it" is verse 11, where again He tells them of Cyrus (45:1) who will come and rescue them from Babylon. This literally happened to prove that God's counsel will stand.

Take time now and thank the Lord for salvation and for carrying you. Unlike man-made means of satisfaction, we can trust God to ultimately deliver us.

wednesday　Isaiah 48:1-11

Digging Deeper • God tells Israel that it knows the right words to claim Him as Lord, yet the people worship idols. All the way from the Exodus (Deuteronomy 28:64), God promised to expel them from the land and to send them into captivity if they disobeyed (v. 3). Now that was happening because of their disobedience. But there was still hope: the "new things" in verse 6 speak about the restoration where the people of Israel return from Babylonian captivity (which they eventually did). God will save the Jews from themselves for His own glory (vv. 9-11). **If God has fulfilled all of these promises, don't you think He can and will keep His promises to you? He has never broken a promise and never will! You can avoid the mistakes Israel made. Don't just claim God as Lord; also obey Him today.**

thursday　Isaiah 48:12-22

Digging Deeper • This passage has God pleading with Israel to listen to Him and acknowledge what Israel already knows is true. The people know He is the first and last (v. 12); that He created the earth (v. 13); that He controls history (v. 14); and that He can make them prosperous (v. 15). In verse 16, He essentially says, "Come on, guys, this is not a secret!" The problem was that although Israel knew God was what was best (v. 17), the people did not listen to His commandments (v. 18). They could have had peace and enjoyed true righteousness. They could have seen their families blessed. But they chose to forget God's greatness in the past (v. 21) and pursue a path that wouldn't bring peace (v. 22). **Are you ignoring any of God's commandments today that He has said will bring you peace or make you more righteous? How will you change this?**

friday Isaiah 49:1-13

Digging Deeper • Chapters 49-57 talk about Christ, the "suffering Servant." The middle verse (Isaiah 53:6) says, "The Lord hath laid on Him the iniquity of us all," pointing toward Christ's saving death. Isaiah 49:3 calls the Messiah "Israel" in order to identify the Messiah with His people. Not only is Jesus presented as humble in verse 5, but He is presented as Savior to the both Jews and the Gentiles.

God's plan to send Christ—and have Him experience all the suffering He had to for us—was thought of long before Christ even came. With this in mind, how can you share God's plan, which is to save all people, with someone today?

saturday Isaiah 49:14-26

Digging Deeper • In Isaiah's day, and later, while the people of Israel were in captivity in Babylon, they felt like God had abandoned them. Sin was the cause of their separation from God. Yet God told them He would never forget them (vv. 15-16). It was as if He had even written them on the palms of His hands. What a personal, loving God we serve! Verses 17-21 tell us that Jerusalem will be so fruitful that the children will overrun the city so that single, old, barren Jerusalem will wonder where they all came from. The final verses tell how the Gentile nation will carry the Jews back to Israel and serve and help them, with the purpose being the whole world knowing God, and that Christ is their Savior.

God does what He does to glorify Himself. We are to live to glorify God. What can you do to live your life today to glorify your Lord?

What is the focus of your life? Isaiah was totally consumed with a holy, loving, powerful Savior. This week you will see Jesus Christ throughout these pages. Ask God for a fresh vision of Himself. As we see Him clearly, our life will take on eternal significance!

prayer focus for this week

the Question — What is the writer saying?

the Answer — How can I apply this to my life?

sunday Isaiah 50:1-11

Digging Deeper • God asks Israel a series of questions He already knows the answers to. He wants to point out His faithfulness and Israel's foolishness. In verse 1, He emphasizes that He didn't divorce Israel or sell her—Israel is in trouble because of her own sins. In verses 2-3, the questions point to God's power over nature. In verse 4, the attention shifts to Christ and His obedience in going to the cross. "Opened mine ear" (v. 5) is a picture of how a slave submitted himself to his master willingly for life. The ear was pierced as a sign of ownership (Exodus 21:6 and Deuteronomy 15:17).

Have you submitted yourself as a bond slave of Jesus Christ? In what ways do you show your obedience to God?

monday Isaiah 51:1-16

Digging Deeper • A series of examples are laid out for Israel to look at in order to remember God's faithfulness. Isaiah says to look to the rock (v. 1). Look at Abraham (v. 2)—see how God took two old people and brought a whole nation out of ruin. God will make Israel like the Garden of Eden one day in the Messianic Kingdom (vv. 3-5). Verses 6–16 tell Israel to trust the God that can be trusted. While the earth and the heavens will be folded up one day like a garment, God's salvation lasts forever (v. 6). Don't worry about men; look at what God did to bring the people of Israel out of Egypt. One day the redeemed will return from captivity to Jerusalem with joy and singing. Don't be afraid of man or the evil one, and never forget God. **Take time today to thank God for caring for you. Thank Him for the promise that He will never forget His people (v. 16).**

tuesday Isaiah 52:1-12

Digging Deeper • God has a history of redeeming His people from captivity. He brought Israel out of Egypt after 430 years of captivity, and He would deliver them from captivity again. The key for Israel was to look to the Lord. To know that God says "I am He" and "it is I" (v. 6) is the most comforting thing we can know when we are in trouble. Verse 7 says beautiful feet brought good news that salvation and deliverance had come. Paul uses this verse in Romans 10:15 to tell us that the soul-winner has beautiful feet, too! The watchman on the wall of Jerusalem (v. 8) will rejoice when these people return home. As those returning from the captivity of sin return to God, He watches as they come and rejoices (v. 12). **God knows right where you are. Are you far way from Him and in captivity to sin? If so, will you make your way back to Him?**

Wednesday Isaiah 52:13 – 53:12

Digging Deeper • Here we have the most graphic Old Testament picture of Christ's sacrifice for us on the cross. Isaiah 52:13-15 tells us how Jesus Christ would be exalted through His death. Verse 15 predicts that Gentiles will be saved while the Jews are in unbelief. Isaiah 53:1-3 tells about Jesus, the suffering servant of God. Jesus was despised by the Jews the same way that they despised someone who desecrated the temple (Daniel 11:21). Verses 4-6 tell us the way He suffered. Verses 7-9 describe how Jesus was submissive to God the Father in death. And finally in verses 10-12, we see the reward Christ received. His reward was our salvation!

Go through this passage verse by verse and thank God for the salvation He provided through Christ.

thursday Isaiah 54:4-17

Digging Deeper • From the time that Isaiah wrote these words around 700 B.C., Israel has not enjoyed this kind of peace and safety. While this time of blessing is in the future for Israel, it also has many precious promises for us who believe in Jesus. Isaiah says not to fear because blessings are coming. God is like a husband who will protect His wife with "great mercy" and "everlasting kindness." Jerusalem will one day be beautiful with precious stones everywhere (vv. 11-12; Revelation 21-22). A wonderful promise for Israel and for you is found in verse 17: "No weapon found against thee shall prosper."

We are told that God's protection is the heritage of the servants of the Lord. Are you serving Him today? Does your righteousness come from God? If so, then why not claim the promise of verse 17 for yourself today?

friday   Isaiah 55:1-13

Digging Deeper • God's way of salvation is always the same throughout all time. Here the eloquent prophet Isaiah presents *God's Invitation of the Ages.* Verses 1-3 present the call to salvation. Who is invited to be saved? Everyone who is thirsty. Verses 6 and 7 show us the process of salvation. Seek the Lord, call on Him (Romans 10:13), then repent of your sins. He will abundantly pardon. Verse 12 tells about the blessings of salvation: joy, peace, and all creation rejoicing with you in your salvation. Look at the wonderful promises of how God will bless Isaiah (vv. 4-5) and His Word (vv. 8-11).
God's salvation, and the blessings that follow, are available to everyone. How—or to whom—can you share God's invitation of the ages today?

saturday   Isaiah 57:15-21

Digging Deeper • We are back on holy ground in today's passage, just as Isaiah was in Isaiah 6:1 when he had his vision of God in the temple. Now, years later, he still sees the high and Holy One who inhabits eternity! What verses 16-19 describe seems to say that we have to do a lot to come before this holy God, but these verses are actually a picture of God seeking us out—not us changing Him! All we have to do is what verse 15 says, which is simply have a contrite and humble spirit. Whether we are near or far, God wants to heal and comfort us. How opposite is the plight of the wicked (vv. 20-21)? There is no peace for them.
Isn't it a relief to know that we don't have to chase God? We just need to be humble before His holiness. Are you at peace, resting in God (vv. 20-21)? If not, how can you practice humility before God today?

Week 42

This week is our seventh and final week on our journey through Isaiah. Have you fallen more deeply in love with Jesus as you have seen the loving heart of our Almighty God revealed through these pages of Holy Scripture? One week to go!

prayer focus for this week

the Question — What is the writer saying?

the Answer — How can I apply this to my life?

sunday Isaiah 58:1-14

Digging Deeper • God is always interested in the heart. Verses 2-7 show us the Jews going through the motions of worship, yet God sees what they are really doing. True religion is to visit the fatherless and the widows—showing concern—and keeping ourselves unspotted from the world (James 1:27). These Jews were not taking care of their own. Instead of feeding their kinsmen, they were exploiting them. But there is hope that they would start doing right for the right reasons. Verses 8-14 describe the blessed life that comes from people doing right because they love God. Isaiah calls it "delighting in the Lord" (v. 14).

Why do you do what you do? Is it because you know you should, or do you do it out of genuine love for God? Ask God to examine your motives—and give you a real love for Him.

monday Isaiah 59:1-2, 12-21

Digging Deeper • God is not limited. He can save with His hand and can hear with His ear, but sin is what always separates man from God (vv. 1-2). Still, when man was at his absolute worst (vv.12-15), then God sent His best by sending the intercessor, the God-man—Jesus Christ—to bridge the gap from sinful man to Holy God. Jesus did this for us on the cross. Not only that, but Jesus will come again (vv.17-21) and appear as a mighty warrior. He will destroy His enemies with great power. When the Redeemer returns to Zion, God's spirit will empower His people.

Our sin has derailed much of our lives on earth, but it hasn't stopped God. He still saves and conquers. Knowing this, who can you talk to who doesn't know Christ? Who do you know who may think they are too deep in sin to ever have a clean life?

tuesday Isaiah 60:1-6, 14-16

Digging Deeper • The most prosperous time in Israel's history was the 40 years that Solomon reigned (971-931 B.C.). But except for a few bright spots, it has been darkness ever since. Christ's public ministry brought great light, but it was rejected. Isaiah tells us that a day is coming when Christ will return and great light will once again return to Israel. Imagine this in light of the chaos and killing going on in Israel today. The Arab nations will bring gifts to Jerusalem and worship the Lord there. Jews will come from all over the earth. God will make Jerusalem an "eternal excellency" and a "joy of many generations."

John concluded the Revelation with the words "even so come Lord Jesus." Pray today for Christ to return. Only then will there be peace in Israel and peace on earth.

wednesday Isaiah 60:19 - 61:3

Digging Deeper • Can you imagine living in a world where God is literally the light? This is what the world will be like during the Millennial Reign of Christ. Everyone will be completely righteous, children will be everywhere, and God will be our Glory (60:19-22). Jesus quoted Isaiah 61:1-20 in Luke 4:16-22 when He visited His hometown synagogue in Nazareth. He proclaimed His deity in this statement. By stopping with "the acceptable year of the Lord" and neglecting to say "and the day of vengeance of our God," He showed both His first and second comings. The vengeance part will happen during the Tribulation Period. Verses 2 and 3 will be fulfilled when all will be saved.

Are you living for the Glory of God? Think of how often this truth is mentioned in Isaiah. Memorize and meditate on Isaiah 61:1-2.

thursday Isaiah 61:7 - 62:5

Digging Deeper • Isaiah 61 talks about the peace that will be in the millennium, and Isaiah 62 tells how God will restore Israel during that time. God is going to give a double portion back to Israel during the millennium, just like Job received double of all he lost (Job 1 and Job 42:12), and a double portion was promised to the firstborn in a Jewish family. The picture here is of a joyful bride and bridegroom. No longer will the woman be called forsaken and desolate, but she will be called Hephzibah ("my delight is in her") and Beulah ("married"). God will rejoice over Israel once more.

Isn't it awesome to think that you have been accepted by the God of the universe? Thank Him for the love that He has for you today.

friday   Psalm 119:105-112

Q my friends / attitude / busyness

A encouraging verses?

Digging Deeper • If you've ever been camping, you know it can be very scary being alone in the woods at night. What can make it even scarier is if clouds cover the moon. Trying to walk when you can't see what's ahead of you can be dangerous—just a little light would help you see your way back. If you were smart, you would have remembered a flashlight to help navigate your way back to the campsite. Walking in this dark world can be just as scary and just as dangerous. You need Christ, Who is the Light of the world, and His Word to help you get home safely. That's why having a daily time in the Word is so important. It will keep you on the path that follows God.

What are some things that keep you from following God? How can God's Word help you walk in a way that will keep you from sinning?

saturday   Psalm 119:113-120

Q

A

Digging Deeper • Do you like making choices? It seems that the more choices there are, the more difficult it is to decide. Restaurant menus can really be a frustration for someone who doesn't like making choices. God's Word offers choices, too. There aren't many choices; in fact, ultimately, there are really only two. The first is to love and obey God and His Word wholeheartedly and enjoy His blessings forever. The second choice is to hate God and choose your own way and experience the consequences of separation from Him forever. The only hope is found in making the first choice. Don't put off making your choice—do it now!

Have you ever made the choice God's Word offers? When? Take the time to write out your testimony and then share it with someone at school or work. Help them make the choice to believe in Christ and follow Him!

Week 46

Wouldn't it be great if the moment you trusted Christ, you were transported to Heaven? Since that didn't happen, God's Word helps you know how to live here while you're waiting for Him to return. Are you ready for some pointers?

prayer focus for this week

the Question — What is the writer saying?

the Answer — How can I apply this to my life?

sunday · Psalm 119:121-128

Q

A

Digging Deeper • Do cheaters frustrate you? Whether it is a game of Monopoly or a game of soccer, if someone tries to win by cheating, it can cause some real problems. The reason is that there are specific rules that are in place to make playing fair for everyone. Once the rules are broken, it is difficult to restore order to the game? But just because others cheat, it doesn't make it right for you to do it. God and His Word must be the absolute authority of right and wrong in your life. If you love Him, you must have the same attitude the psalmist had in verse 128 – hatred for every false way!

Do you hate evil the way God does? Can you think of a time this week when you did not hate evil enough to stay away from it? Have you asked God to forgive you?

monday   Psalm 119:129-136

Digging Deeper • Have you ever had a craving for a particular food that no substitute could satisfy? Maybe it was a favorite meal that your mom hadn't made in a while or a particular ice cream that was no longer available. No other food could satisfy that craving, and the more you thought about it, the stronger the desire became. That's the kind of craving David had for God and His Word. He felt parched and unfulfilled until God's Word quenched his thirst. He desired to live in a way that pleased God. You and I can open God's Word any time for the answers to life's problems, but we sometimes neglect it for weeks. We need to thirst for God like David did.

Is knowing God and His Word the desire of your heart? Do you hunger to know Him more? Ask God to give you that hunger.

tuesday   Psalm 119:137-144

Digging Deeper • Are you a sports fanatic? Do you eat, sleep, and breathe sports? Do you know all the statistics about every player on a team? Maybe just the mention of your team or a player excites you. That is zeal! That's similar to the way the psalmist felt about God. He says in verse 139 that "his zeal consumed him"; in other words his whole life was focused on knowing and pleasing God! What would it take for your zeal for God to exceed your zeal for your favorite sport? One way that would help is by being faithful daily to do what you are doing right now—a quiet time. Just as your zeal for that sport needed time to develop, so does your zeal for the Lord. The more you stay in His Word, the more zealous for Him you will become.

Will you commit to spend part of every day getting to know God? Find someone who will keep you accountable about your decision.

wednesday Psalm 119:145-152

Digging Deeper • When do you call out to God in prayer? Is it only at mealtimes or before you go to sleep? Is it only when you need help on a big test or have a problem? Are they half-hearted or short prayers? How you pray and what you pray about is a reflection of where your heart is. In today's passage, David put his entire body into his prayers; it affected his life. He literally cried out to God day and night. His desire to have God's answers caused him to lose sleep and maybe a meal or two. He wasn't too concerned about time (vv. 147-148); it was more important to spend time in prayer. He may have been ridiculed (v. 150), but that didn't matter. **How is your prayer life? Write out your prayers to God for the next week in a journal and try to discover if your heart is as zealous for God as David's was. You may be surprised at what you learn.**

thursday Psalm 119:153-160

Digging Deeper • One thing that knowing God and His Word should do is give you a clear understanding of right and wrong. The more you learn, the more sensitive to sin's deception you should be. You'll begin to see people as God does—lost and destined for His judgment, or saved and bound for Heaven (v. 155). You'll understand that being a Christian is more than just a name; it should affect everything you do (v. 156). It will keep you from giving into pressure from people because your goal in life should be to please God above all else (v. 157). **Have you made up your mind about living for God? Do you have friends who need to know Christ's love and salvation? Add their names to your daily prayer diary and pray for them. Don't forget to share the Gospel with them.**

friday   Psalm 119:161-168

Digging Deeper • Imagine that you received a DVD in the mail with instructions to invite your family and closest friends to watch it with you. That evening, everyone sits in the living room, stuffing his or her face with popcorn as you begin the movie. Two minutes into the program, you realize someone has secretly taped every move you made over the past month—everything! Are you nervous or embarrassed at what the others are seeing, or quietly confident that you've done all right? In a very real sense, the psalmist is saying that every move we make is on display before God (v. 168). How does that make you feel? Look how it affected David—it kept him from sin.

How will your life and activities change, knowing that God's eyes are on you? What changes need to be made in your life?

saturday   Psalm 119:169-176

Digging Deeper • Do you ever find yourself repeating the same mistake or giving into the same temptation again and again? You're not alone. Even after writing this entire psalm, recognizing the power of God's Word to keep him from sin, look how David described himself in verse 176. Sheep are prone to wander if they do not follow their shepherd closely. They are easily distracted. We are very similar to sheep because we often wander. Thank God that He is the Good Shepherd who seeks out His own and doesn't leave us when we wander. If you've learned anything as you've studied this psalm, it should be that you can trust God's Word to put you on the right path.

What are the things that cause you to wander from God? List three things that you've learned about God in your study of Psalm 119.

"Excuses, excuses, excuses, that's all I ever hear!" Have you ever heard those words from your mom or dad after they asked you to clean your room, take out the trash, or do your homework and you didn't? This week we'll see why those who reject God's righteousness through Jesus Christ have no excuse.

prayer focus for this week

the Question   **What is the writer saying?**

the Answer   **How can I apply this to my life?**

sunday   Romans 1:1-7

Q

A

Digging Deeper • Paul introduces us to the main character of the entire book of Romans in the first six words of verse 1: Jesus Christ. Paul identifies himself as the servant of Jesus Christ, or literally, *the slave who chose to be so when he could have gone free*. That's kind of like choosing to stay in high school for a few extra years instead of graduating, only much more. Because of what Christ did for him, Paul wants to serve Him for the rest of his life, for the glory of God. We can have the same attitude, because Jesus Christ did the same things for us that He did for Paul. The highlight of what Christ did for us was Him showing us His power by rising from the dead (v. 4). It's called the resurrection, proving He is the Son of God.
What specific things does Paul tell us that Jesus Christ did for us? What specific things are you doing that show you are His servant?

monday   Romans 1:8-17

Digging Deeper • Did you ever have a friend or family member move away, and you wanted to see them so badly that you prayed and asked God to make it possible for you to go visit them? Paul prayed that God would allow him to visit the Roman believers so that he could support them in their walk with God. He wanted to see them so that together they could be comforted, encouraged, and strengthened by each other's faith. Paul's desire to share the Gospel with those who hadn't yet believed was so strong that he described it as a debt that he owed them. He was committed to preach the Gospel with every ounce of strength he had, because he knew that once he shared, God's power would bring salvation to all who would believe.
Ask God to burden your heart for one Christian friend who you can encourage, and one unsaved friend with whom you can share the Gospel.

tuesday   Romans 1:18-32

Digging Deeper • Have you ever shared the Gospel with an unbeliever who argued that God couldn't possibly send people to Hell if they had never heard the Gospel? Verse 20 makes it very clear that they have no excuse! God's creation speaks loud and clear and tells us that there is a God. If anyone wants to know the truth, they just have to open their eyes! We're also told that God "gave them up" (vv. 24, 26) and that He "gave them over" (v. 28). That doesn't mean that God gave up on them, but that because they refused to accept God's truth, He let them go their own way and suffer the consequences. Anyone can know the truth if they want to.
Many people argue with God's way, making excuses for how they think life should be. Using this passage, write out your answer to the question, "How can God send someone to Hell who hasn't heard the Gospel?"

wednesday Romans 2:1-16

Digging Deeper • Imagine that you are driving your car, and every other car on the road is passing you. You decide to go faster, and before you know it, you are being pulled over for speeding. You tell the policeman that everyone else was speeding, and therefore, he shouldn't give you a ticket. Then he tells you, "That's no excuse!" God will judge all men according to His truth, His standard. He tells those who point their fingers at others who are sinning that they have to answer for their own actions. For those who remain "impenitent" (v. 5—no repentance), they will be judged according to their deeds.

Do you ever do things that you know are wrong, pointing at everyone else who is doing the same thing? Write down some specific areas where you know you should change. How can you make this right with God?

thursday Romans 2:17-29

Digging Deeper • "Practice what you preach!" Have you heard those words before? They are typically used when referring to someone who tells people not to act a certain way, but then acts that way himself. We call that person a hypocrite. Paul was a Jew, and now he is talking to the Jews, who were known for their hypocrisy. They argued that they were keeping the Law when, in fact, they were just "going through the motions" and actually violating the very laws that they taught others. Obedience comes from the heart, not from mere outward conformity.

Write a brief sentence or two that describes your motivation for going to church or having your quiet time. What words would God use to describe your heart? Could any of your actions be a good reason for someone to call you a hypocrite? Why?

friday Romans 3:1-8

Digging Deeper • Have you ever wondered what it would be like to be the son or daughter of the President? Just think about the places you could go and the things you could do simply because your dad was in charge. I don't think you would ever question whether or not your family gave you an advantage over other people. The Jews had that kind of advantage; they were God's chosen people and were given the "oracles" (v. 2), or *the very words of God*. Yet with all the advantages they had, they still refused to put their faith in Jesus Christ and His promise of salvation. As a result, they will be judged by God for their unbelief.

List the advantages you have as a result of being a child of God. How have you used those advantages to proclaim His truth?

saturday Romans 3:9-20

Digging Deeper • Sometimes when unsaved people are presented with the Gospel, and they are told that they are sinners, their response may go something like this: "Sure, I've sinned. Who hasn't? But hey, I'm not that bad. After all, I haven't killed anyone. I do enough good things. It'll come out all right in the end." God's answer is, "There is none that seeketh after God…there is none that doeth good" (vv. 11-12). In other words, no man can ever be good enough to overcome his guilt. Even keeping the Law (commandments) will not justify anyone. The Law is intended to show us how sinful and unrighteous we are, not to make us better.

Put Paul's description of all men into your own words. How does that make you feel? What hope do we have?

Week 48

Have you ever been so lost that you were overwhelmed by fear and just about to give up hope of ever finding your way, when suddenly someone you knew showed up and rescued you? Last week's study ended with no hope. This week we will learn about God's answer to man's hopelessness!

prayer focus for this week

 the **Question**   What is the writer saying?

 the **Answer**   How can I apply this to my life?

sunday   Romans 3:21-31

Q

A

Digging Deeper • Debt is a way of life in the United States. If we want something and don't have the money to buy it, we borrow the money and get what we want. Some people have borrowed so much money that they have no hope of ever getting out of debt. Because we are all sinners, we owe God a debt that we can never pay. But God made it possible for our debt to be *paid in full* by receiving His righteousness through faith in Jesus Christ. It's not about doing the works of the Law, but accepting the blood of Christ as the payment for our sin.

This passage contains many theological words directly related to our salvation. Make a list of those words and what they mean. If necessary, use a Bible dictionary to help you with the definitions.

monday Romans 4:1-12

Digging Deeper • I'll believe it when I see it!" That's how we respond when something we think is impossible actually happens. There are some things in life that we just have to accept as true without seeing them, like electricity or gravity. Have you ever seen either one? Of course not, but you believe that they exist, don't you? We can only experience the righteousness of God by believing Him. We can't earn it or get it through doing good things or following the Law, which is what the Jews were doing through circumcision. Even Old Testament heroes like Abraham and David had to exercise faith in order to receive God's grace and forgiveness.
Is faith really all that is necessary to receive God's righteousness? How do you know? Write out your salvation story and share it with a friend who knows the Lord, and with one who doesn't.

tuesday Romans 4:13-25

Digging Deeper • Luke 1:37 tells us, "For with God nothing shall be impossible." That means a man can live for three days in the belly of a great fish (Jonah 1:17), a baby can be born to a virgin (Luke 1:34-35), or a baby can be born to a 100-year-old man and a ninety-year-old woman (Genesis 17:17). "Nothing" means "nothing!" Abraham didn't "stagger" (v. 20) or doubt God's promise to give him a son, no matter how old he was. As a result, he received God's righteousness. God's righteousness is also available to us because of another seeming impossibility…that Jesus died on the cross and rose from the dead (vv. 24-25). Because God did the impossible, you and I can believe and be saved!
For what impossible things have you believed God in the past? Make a list of impossible things for which you want to begin to ask God in the future.

wednesday   Romans 5:1-11

Digging Deeper • The end of any war has always been a cause for celebration because it brought peace and hope to those who were set free from the enemy. For those of us who have been "justified by faith" (v. 1), we now have peace with God. We were once guilty before God and slaves to sin, but now we are free and at peace with Him. That peace also gives us access to God anytime we want it. Peace leads to rejoicing, hope, and the pouring out of God's love in our hearts. Talk about a reason for celebration—we've got a whole bunch of reasons to be thankful and give glory to God!

When's the last time you celebrated your peace with God? Write a prayer to God praising Him for setting you free from sin and giving you peace.

thursday   Romans 5:12-21

Digging Deeper • The story of sin entering the human race through Adam and Eve is a familiar one. It may be easy to think that if we could have taken their place in the Garden, we wouldn't have sinned. The truth of the matter is that we all sinned in Adam, and that means that we would have done the same thing. But just as sin entered the world through one man, so by the obedience of one man, Jesus Christ, all can be made righteous. The sin of one brought death to all, and the death of one brought God's grace and forgiveness to all. Sin is powerful and deadly. But the gift of salvation is more powerful than sin and brings life.

Think about the sins you've committed in the last week. Write them on a piece of paper, confess them to God (1 John 1:9), and then shred them. You have been forgiven!

friday  Romans 6:1-12

Digging Deeper • Baptism is a picture of our salvation. When we are baptized, we identify with Christ in His death and burial by being put under the water. When we are raised up out of the water, we identify with Him in His resurrection. The picture is that we are buried to sin and raised up to new life in Christ. As believers, we don't have to sin. Talk about hope—this is more than hope; it is freedom from sin—it is victory! Sin can no longer control us because we are alive in Christ.

Have you been baptized? If not, why not? How will you publicly identify yourself with Jesus Christ this week? List one thing you can do to let your friends see the life of Christ in you.

saturday Romans 6:13-23

Digging Deeper • What controls you? To what do you give your time each day? Is it sports, a musical instrument, or a part in the school play? If so, you must commit your time to long hours of practice or rehearsal. You must willingly give yourself to your team and the coach, to your instrument, or to the director. In the same way, if you want to have victory over sin, you must give your time and effort to doing those things that please God. If you spend your time on things that are not pleasing to God, you will become a slave to those things. Remember, "The wages (penalty) of sin is death, but the gift of God is eternal life" (v. 23). Live your life for God!

Is sin controlling you? How? Are there friends or activities you need to get rid of in order to avoid sin and be closer to God? Who or what are they? What do you need to do today to give yourself to God?

Week 49

Do you sometimes struggle with this thing we call "the Christian life"? Why is it so hard? Why do we do the things that we hate? Why do bad things happen to good people? Why does it seem that at times God is unfair? Why, why, why? You will find some answers this week, but you might also discover some more questions!

prayer focus for this week

the Question — What is the writer saying?

the Answer — How can I apply this to my life?

sunday   Romans 7:1-13

Q

A

Digging Deeper • Have you ever been to a wedding? Did you actually listen to what the pastor said when he asked the bride and groom to repeat their vows? Do you remember the part about "for as long as you both shall live" and "until death do us part"? That means that the only thing that should end a marriage is death. And just as death is the only thing that ends a marriage, so our relationship with Christ is the only thing that can make us dead to the law. Once we are dead to the law, we are no longer bound to or controlled by the law, but we are set free to live and serve in the Spirit.

Marriage changes your life. How has your salvation, your marriage to Christ, changed your life? Share three specific examples.

monday Romans 7:14-25

Digging Deeper • Count how many times the word I is used in these verses. That's right, a lot. "For the good that I would I do not: but the evil which I would not, that I do" (v. 19). What in the world is Paul trying to tell us? I, I, I…me, me, me. Even as a believer, Paul identifies himself as "carnal" (v. 14). Carnal means "subject to the weaknesses of the human flesh." Even though we are saved and don't have to sin, the struggle against sin—and a life dominated by thoughts of ourselves—still exists. It sounds like Paul is almost ready to give up and give in to sin when he exclaims, "O wretched (miserable) man that I am! Who shall deliver me?" (v. 24). Is there any hope? Yes, it is through Jesus Christ our Lord (v. 25).
When do you struggle most to overcome sin? What sin do you struggle with the most? Are you focused on "I," or on Jesus Christ?

tuesday Romans 8:1-11

Digging Deeper • I'm sure you've seen TV shows that take place in a courtroom. The evidence is presented, and the jury decides the guilt or innocence of the defendant. If the words "not guilty" are heard, everyone shouts for joy and celebrates because there is "no condemnation" for the defendant. The words "no condemnation" are also true for everyone who is in Christ Jesus. We have been set free from sin and death because God's own Son became our sin offering. We can now live in the power of the Spirit of God because we have been forgiven and made alive!
How do you celebrate the fact that we cannot be condemned? According to these verses, what part does the Spirit play in our salvation and spiritual growth?

wednesday Romans 8:12-25

Digging Deeper • The relationship a father has with his son or daughter is very special. A father would do anything for his child, and that child experiences special blessings from his or her father that no one else will get. For those of us who have been made alive by Christ Jesus and led by the Spirit, we are now "sons of God" (vv. 14-15). We have entered into a new relationship because we have been adopted into the family of God and now cry out "Abba, Father" (v. 15). As God's children, we have been given an inheritance and a hope for the present and the future. One day God's glory will be revealed in us as we stand in His presence for all eternity.

How would you rate your relationship with your heavenly Father? Do you know Him well enough to call Him "Father" when you pray? Why?

thursday Romans 8:26-39

Digging Deeper • What do you say to someone who has just experienced the death of a friend or loved one? In our desire to help, we may say something insensitive. Sometimes, the grief is so deep that we don't know what to say. We may not even know how to pray for hurting people. That's when the Holy Spirit "intercedes" for us by taking our groanings and unspoken words to our Father on our behalf (v. 26). It's during those times that we usually ask, "Why did this happen?" The answer is that God works "all things" together to accomplish His will and purpose in our lives (v. 28). We may not understand what that purpose is, but we can be confident that God will use it for our good and to bring honor and glory to Himself.

Is there hurt in your life today? Are you facing difficult circumstances and wondering what to do? Go to God now and cry out to Him for wisdom.

friday   Romans 9:1-16

Digging Deeper • How much do you know about Israel? What about Palestine? What is all the fighting about in the Middle East? The Jews are still God's chosen people even though God has turned His attention to the church today. Paul's heart is broken for his fellow countrymen, the Jews. They have rejected Christ as the Messiah, and Paul wishes that he could be "accursed" (v. 3) in their place. In other words, he is willing to take their eternal punishment in Hell if it would mean that they would be saved. Jacob and Esau are mentioned to illustrate God's truth about election. God loved (chose) Jacob and hated (rejected) Esau. For more about Esau, look at Hebrews 12:14-17 to see why Esau was not accepted by God.

How burdened is your heart for your unsaved friends? How much would you do to reach them for Christ? When will you do it?

saturday   Romans 9:17-33

Digging Deeper • "That's not fair!" is a phrase that comes out of our mouths when someone gets something that we didn't get, and we view it as preferential treatment. It might be a complaint verbalized by teenagers to parents, by students to teachers, or by believers to God. When we see God's mercy shown to one and not another, we may think that's unfair. But Paul asks in v. 20, "Who are you to reply against God?" God is the potter and we are the clay, and the clay can never question the potter's right to do what he wants! Ultimately, God does what He does to bring glory to Himself, and fairness is never the issue.

Have you been angry at God for treating you or someone else unfairly? Why? What do you need to change about how you think about God?

Week 50

We begin this week with two of the most used salvation verses in the entire Bible: Romans 10:9-10. God's righteousness for all men, Jew or Gentile, comes only by believing and confessing. Once we're saved, the reasonable outcome is to present our bodies as a sacrifice to God and to serve Him and one another.

prayer focus for this week

the **Question**   **What is the writer saying?**

the **Answer**   **How can I apply this to my life?**

sunday   Romans 10:1-13

Q

A

Digging Deeper • Israel had a zeal for God, but not according to knowledge (v. 2). Being ignorant of God's righteousness, the people of Israel zealously tried to earn their own way, but they were not able to obey the 613 commandments in the Mosaic Code. They would need a Savior. Because of Christ's sinless life, He became the end or fulfillment of the Law (v. 4) and was the only one eligible to pay the wages of sin for us (6:23). Two very familiar verses used when witnessing to the unsaved are verses 9-10. They talk about confessing with our mouth, and believing with our heart when it comes to Christ's death, burial, and resurrection. God meets man's greatest need in verse 13: For whosoever shall call... (Prayer) ...upon the name of the Lord... (Person) ...shall be saved (Personal Relationship). Have you done this yet? Do you know of others who need to do this?

monday Romans 10:14-21

Digging Deeper • Jesus tells us in Matthew 9:37-38 that the "harvest truly is plenteous (great), but the laborers are few." There is a huge need for people to give themselves to lifetime ministry and to take the Gospel into the worldwide harvest. Paul tells us that those in need of the Gospel can't believe if they never hear, and they can't hear if someone doesn't preach to them. It's real simple— faith (the ability to believe) can only come as the lost (the great harvest field of people who don't know the Lord Jesus) hear the Word of God. And they can only hear it if we are willing to take it to them.

What are you doing to reach the world for Christ? Have you considered a lifetime in ministry? How can you share God's message of hope to people you run into every day?

tuesday Romans 11:1-12

Digging Deeper • Did you see today's biggest headline? It read, "God Rejects the Nation of Israel!" No, not really, but today's text begins with a question that could easily be turned into a major news story, if it were true. However, God has not rejected His people, the Jews. Unfortunately, *Israel* has rejected Jesus as the Messiah and keeps trying to gain its own righteousness by the works of the Law. As a result, God put the people of Israel aside for a time so He could work with Gentiles who choose to come to Him, now known as the *Church* or the *Bride of Christ*. God will turn to Israel again during the Tribulation period and give those people another opportunity to respond favorably to Him by placing their faith and trust in Him.

What can people see in your life that indicates *you* have not rejected Jesus Christ as the Messiah?

wednesday Romans 11:13-24

Digging Deeper • Have you ever read a passage of Scripture, struggled to understand it, read it a second time, and then wondered what it really meant? Today's text requires some thought, prayer, and study. The Gentiles (v. 13) are the church, and Paul's "flesh" (v. 14) is the Jews. The "firstfruit" and "root" (v. 16) refer to the start of Israel through Abraham, Isaac, and Jacob. The branches that are "broken off" (v. 17) are the Jews who rejected Jesus as Messiah, and "the wild olive tree" (v. 17) is the church. God treated the Jews with "severity or sternness" because of their unbelief, and believing Gentiles with "goodness" because of their faith (vv. 20, 22). Our response ought to be one of fear, humility, and ultimately thanksgiving for our salvation!

When you think of what God has done for you, how do you respond?

thursday Romans 11:25-36

Digging Deeper • Almost everyone likes a good mystery. Whether it's a book, a TV show, or video, it's always a challenge to work through the plot and try to figure out who did it. In verse 25, the "mystery" (something not revealed in the Old Testament) is that God would set aside Israel for a time to work with the Gentiles (the church) until the "fullness of the Gentiles" is complete. The "fullness" refers to the entire number of Gentiles that God intends to save as part of the church. When the last Gentile is saved, Jesus Christ will return for His church at the Rapture, and the seven years of Tribulation will begin.

How do you know that you are ready for the Rapture? Knowing that the fullness of the Gentiles may happen at any moment, will you change the way you are living right now?

friday   Romans 12:1-8

Digging Deeper • Can you remember a time when you wanted to get even with someone because of what he or she did to you? Have you ever thought about *getting even* with God, because of what He did *for* you? Now, we can never really get even with God or pay Him back because of all that He has done for us. But we can "present [offer] our bodies a living sacrifice" (v. 1) to God, so that He can accomplish His will in our lives. When we take that step, we are then ready to use the "gifts" (special God-given abilities for service—v. 6) to minister to other members of the body of Christ.

What are you doing now to make your life a living sacrifice to God? What "gifts" has God given you for serving Him? How are you developing and using those gifts?

saturday   Romans 12:9-21

Digging Deeper • "They're all a bunch of hypocrites!" is a phrase often used in reference to the church. Paul gives us a list of practical tips for daily living that will reflect the righteousness of God in our lives and help people see that we can live like the God we say we believe in. Verse 9 alludes directly to hypocrisy when it says love is without "dissimulation," a word that comes from the ancient Greek theatrical practice of having actors wear masks for different parts in the play and, as a result, hiding their true identity. Paul's command is telling us not to speak "from under a mask in order to deceive." If we learn to "love one another" first, the rest of the list will be easy.

Are you a hypocrite? Look at these verses to find specific areas with which you may struggle. What do you need to change?

Week 51

Life is all about relationships! In fact, after telling us to love the Lord with all our heart, Jesus tells us to love our neighbors as we love ourselves (Matthew 22:39). This week we will learn about the value of people and how to live at peace with all men, whether saved or unsaved, weak or strong, Jew or Gentile.

prayer focus for this week

the Question What is the writer saying?

the Answer How can I apply this to my life?

sunday Romans 13:1-14

Q

A

Digging Deeper • Periodically, a country elects a new political leader, and whether we agree with the outcome of the election, we are to submit to the government that God has established. The key is to remember that God is sovereign and the ultimate authority in our country. We are to obey our earthly rulers, not only because of possible punishment, but also because of our conscience before God. We keep the law by obeying the speed limit, not shoplifting, and telling the truth. But we also keep the law by loving our neighbor like we love ourselves. When we love our neighbor that way, the rest of the commandments will take care of themselves.

How often do you pray for our elected officials? What is your motivation for obeying different laws? What are you doing to love those around you?

monday Romans 14:1-12

Digging Deeper • If we could learn to make Christ first and our desires last on a daily basis, we would never think of "despising"—or judging—one another (vv. 3-4, 10). These verses deal with the gray areas of life. The specific issue at hand is whether or not a Christian should eat meat offered to idols. One believer eats and the other (the weak brother—a new or immature believer) doesn't. Neither is wrong, and neither are to judge the other. Both are to live for the Lord because God is the judge and will hold each one accountable.

What gray areas do you argue about with other Christians? Are you critical of them? What does today's passage say about that? What Biblical basis do you have for the things that you believe?

tuesday Romans 14:13-23

Digging Deeper • If your mom made dinner tonight with meat that had been offered to idols, would you eat it? Now, that's probably not a realistic possibility. But what if watching a DVD in front of one of your friends would cause him to "stumble" (vv.13, 21)—that is, to sin? Would you watch it anyway? You may think, "That's ridiculous. What's wrong with watching a DVD? That's not a sin!" No, it's not—unless it causes your friend to sin because his convictions tell him not to watch it. A bit extreme? Maybe, but it's exactly the kind of thing that Paul is talking about. Whatever the issue, let's not "destroy" (v. 15) our brother by doing what we think is okay. We need to pursue things that lead to spiritual growth.

What are you doing that leads to the spiritual growth of other believers? What activity would you give up for the sake of a weaker brother?

wednesday   Romans 15:1-13

Digging Deeper • Would you consider yourself to be a weak or strong believer? Most of us would like to think that we are strong, but how do we know for sure? Paul gives us a foolproof test. Those who are strong "ought to," or actually are duty-bound to, "bear the infirmities (weaknesses) of the weak" (v. 1) and to "please his neighbour for his good" (v. 2). It couldn't be clearer. Mature believers are to live for the glory of God and the good of others, for even Christ chose not to please Himself. We are to accept one another just as Christ accepted us and be "like-minded" (v. 5) toward each other.

Does God consider you to be a strong believer? What are you doing to help those you know in school, at work, or in your youth group? How have you specifically chosen not to please yourself for the good of someone else?

thursday   Romans 15:14-33

Digging Deeper • Ben Franklin said, "It's amazing what can be accomplished when no one cares who gets the credit." We live in a society that makes a big deal about who gets the credit, yet Paul said God should get all the recognition. Paul was greatly used of God to take the Gospel to the Gentiles, from Jerusalem to central Europe, and all the way to Spain. He was an amazing servant of God. Yet he showed who he really served by caring first that the people heard the Gospel. Paul shows his dependence on God by asking for the prayers of the Roman church for his ministry in Jerusalem, Judea, and Rome. When we learn to depend on God, we also learn that He deserves the credit for all that takes place.

What is God doing in your life for which you are taking the credit? What more could you do if you cared only that God got the credit?

f𝐫ida𝐲   Romans 16:1-16

Digging Deeper • Do you remember this week's overview? Relationships have been at the heart of everything that Paul has said in the last four chapters of his letter to the church at Rome. Are you a friendly person? Paul was. As a result, he had a lot of friends. He greets twenty-eight people by name in chapter 16. He didn't just know their names, but in many cases, he knew very specific details about them. This only comes through spending time with them. It would also seem to indicate that he didn't seek to please himself, but that he had actually built some lasting relationships with them and sought to encourage his brothers and sisters in Christ everywhere he went.
How well do you know those you see in everyday life? What are you doing to get to know them so that you can pray for them specifically?

satu𝐫da𝐲   Romans 16:17-27

Digging Deeper • Paul closes the last section of his letter with a warning to mark (v. 17), or watch out for, those who cause divisions within the church that are contrary to the doctrines they have been taught. He says to stay away from them. Relationships with disobedient people can be devastating to the church and the testimony of Jesus Christ. Paul ends his letter the way he began it—with an emphasis on the grace of God and the person of the Lord Jesus Christ. We would do well to make sure that there is always a constant emphasis on the grace of God and the Lord Jesus Christ in our lives!
Are you spending time with those who are living contrary to the truth of the Word of God? Why? What does the grace of God mean to you? How does your life reflect the presence of the Lord Jesus Christ?

Week 52

The story of Hosea, the Prophet, and Gomer, his harlot wife, is one of the greatest love stories in the Bible. It is a picture of God's love for unfaithful Israel. Once the story has been told in the first two chapters, we will look at Hosea's message to Israel and us in the rest of the book.

prayer focus for this week

the Question — What is the writer saying?

the Answer — How can I apply this to my life?

sunday — Hosea 3:4 – 4:11

Q

A

Digging Deeper • Do you ever wonder if your sin will truly find you out, or if a Holy God will ever punish wicked people? Hosea's prophesies of God judging unfaithful Israel were fulfilled about sixty years later, starting with the captivity of Israel in 722 B.C. and later the captivity of Judah in 586 B.C. The national sin of no truth, no mercy, and no knowledge of God in the land (4:1), and the judgment of verse 5 are blamed on the priests first (vv. 4-8) and also on the people (vv. 9-14).

It takes a long process of wicked thinking to end up in such a tragic position as Israel. What are you doing today to keep yourself from idolatry—letting other things have first place in your life, before God? Pray and ask God to reveal areas of idolatry in your life.

monday   Hosea 4:16 – 5:10

Digging Deeper • "Backslidden" is a term used for Christians who are not living for Jesus more today than they were yesterday. This idea shows up in today's passage. The Lord is the Good Shepherd Who wants to lead us to green pastures. But Israel was behaving like an untrained, half-grown cow that is stuck in the mud and will not unlock her front legs so she can be led out of the mud. Instead she *backslides* further into the mud. Now the rulers (4:18) are in on the sin and God's judgment is in full swing. They refuse to change their ways (5:4), and God now withdraws Himself from them (5:6). Only judgment, signified by the blowing of the trumpet (5:8), will save these people who are out of bounds (5:10).

Are you backslidden today? Are you living for Jesus more today than one month or one week ago? Romans 6:13 has a great remedy if you're not!

tuesday   Hosea 5:14 - 6:6

Digging Deeper • Did you ever see a person who had to hit rock bottom before they returned to the Lord? God is willing to tear His people like a lion (5:14; 6:5) and then wait for their cry. God's tough love is always meant to draw us into a face-to-face love relationship with Him. His call is always "come, and let us return to the Lord." Sometimes the words of the prophets (v. 5) are enough to bring us back to Him. God loves to show us mercy, more than He desires us to bring a sacrifice for our sins!

Even though these verses are rich with meaning for the history of Israel, they have personal application to us. Do you see the great heart of love that God has for us? Won't you live today to please your Savior? What can you do to show Him that you love Him?

wednesday Hosea 10:9-15

Digging Deeper • Have you ever heard the saying, "You reap what you sow"? God's laws of sowing and reaping are in effect in every generation. In Hosea 8:7, we see that Israel has sown to the wind and will reap the whirlwind. In Hosea 9:7, we see that there will be a time when judgment will come. Hosea 10:9 compares Israel's present sin to one of the vilest sins ever recorded in Scripture (Judges 19-20). That sin resulted in a whole tribe of Israel nearly being wiped out. Verse 12 in today's passage tells us that God's laws of sowing and reaping are also positive. "Sow for yourselves righteousness; reap in mercy."

You can choose to be under either God's judgment or mercy. Will you choose your way (v. 13), or will you agree with God that it is "time to seek the Lord" (v. 12)? Ask God for a tender heart today and love what He loves.

thursday Hosea 11:1-9

Digging Deeper • Our God is a God of love. He tells the story of loving Israel in the early days of its nationhood as He called the people out of Egypt. His treatment of Israel helps us see how He cares for His children. God always calls His children to come out of the world and be separate. He draws us with bands of love. He never wants to judge us but always wants us close to Him as obedient children. He never wants judgment to come as it did on Admah and Zeboiim (cities that were judged with Sodom and Gomorrah). Since we are His children, He puts off judgment as long as He can.

What have you said to your loving Father today? Does He know that you love Him like He loves you? Have you thanked Him for His patience toward you today?

friday · Hosea 13:4-14

Digging Deeper • God continues throughout history to pursue Israel. He desires that we worship Him alone, and He will continually pursue us so that we, who have destroyed ourselves with our sins, will find our help in Him. Verses 7 and 8 parallel Daniel's vision in Daniel 7:3-7 where God uses four world empires to draw Israel to Himself. God will be the King of Israel one day.

Is God your King today? Have you seen the hand of God in your circumstances as He draws you to Himself? Even Paul picked up on the note of victory in Hosea 13:14 and gave us the great victory verses of 1 Corinthians 15:54-55. Let's live today in Christ's victory over death and the grave!

saturday · Hosea 14:1-9

Digging Deeper • Hosea proved that his words were true with his life. As an honorable husband to an unfaithful wife, he lived out God's message of love for sinful, backsliding mankind. His message concludes with the words, "return unto the Lord thy God." Verse 2 says that the way to get right with God is our words. Tell the Lord you have sinned (1 John 1:9), and He will forgive you. Use your lips to praise Him (Hebrews 13:15). Great joy and prosperity come to us as the Lord loves us freely, and we respond to His love with fruitful lives. When we hear Him and obey Him, we will be truly prosperous.

Why not pray right now and commit yourself to the Lord in a new and fresh way? Let's ask God to allow us to love Him freely just as He loves us.

The following chart is provided to enable everyone using Word of Life Quiet Times to stay on the same passages. This list also aligns with the daily radio broadcasts.

Week 1	Aug 29 - Sep 4	Psalms 104:1-105:45
Week 2	Sep 5 - Sep 11	Psalms 106:1-108:13
Week 3	Sep 12 - Sep 18	Psalms 109:1-113:9
Week 4	Sep 19 - Sep 25	2 Corinthians 1:1-4:18
Week 5	Sep 26 - Oct 2	2 Corinthians 5:1-8:24
Week 6	Oct 3 - Oct 9	2 Corinthians 9:1-13:14
Week 7	Oct 10 - Oct 16	1 Samuel 1:1-9:27
Week 8	Oct 17 - Oct 23	1 Samuel 10:1-17:16
Week 9	Oct 24 - Oct 30	1 Samuel 17:17-20:42
Week 10	Oct 31 - Nov 6	2 Samuel 5:1-23:7
Week 11	Nov 7 - Nov 13	James 1:1-3:10
Week 12	Nov 14 - Nov 20	James 3:11-5:20
Week 13	Nov 21 - Nov 27	Proverbs 21:1-23:25
Week 14	Nov 28 - Dec 4	Proverbs 23:26-25:28
Week 15	Dec 5 - Dec 11	1 Peter 1:1-3:7
Week 16	Dec 12 - Dec 18	1 Peter 3:8-5:14
Week 17	Dec 19 - Dec 25	Luke 1:1-2:14
Week 18	Dec 26 - Jan 1	Luke 2:15-4:15
Week 19	Jan 2 - Jan 8	Luke 4:16-6:26
Week 20	Jan 9 - Jan 15	Luke 6:27-8:15
Week 21	Jan 16 - Jan 22	Luke 8:16-9:50
Week 22	Jan 23 - Jan 29	Luke 9:51-11:28
Week 23	Jan 30 - Feb 5	Luke 11:29-13:9
Week 24	Feb 6 - Feb 12	Luke 13:10-15:32
Week 25	Feb 13 - Feb 19	Luke 16:1-18:43
Week 26	Feb 20 - Feb 26	Luke 19:1-21:4

Week 27	Feb 27 - Mar 5	Luke 21:5-23:12
Week 28	Mar 6 - Mar 12	Luke 23:13-24:53
Week 29	Mar 13 - Mar 19	Ezekiel 1:1-11:25
Week 30	Mar 20 - Mar 26	Ezekiel 12:17-20:16
Week 31	Mar 27 - Apr 2	Ezekiel 20:17-33:20
Week 32	Apr 3 - Apr 9	Ezekiel 33:21-37:14
Week 33	Apr 10 - Apr 16	Ezekiel 37:15-47:12
Week 34	Apr 17 - Apr 23	Philippians 1:1-2:23
Week 35	Apr 24 - Apr 30	Philippians 2:24-4:23
Week 36	May 1 - May 7	Isaiah 1:1-9:7
Week 37	May 8 - May 14	Isaiah 10:16-26:21
Week 38	May 15 - May 21	Isaiah 28:5-35:10
Week 39	May 22 - May 28	Isaiah 40:1-44:24
Week 40	May 29 - Jun 4	Isaiah 45:5-49:26
Week 41	Jun 5 - Jun 11	Isaiah 50:1-57:21
Week 42	Jun 12 - Jun 18	Isaiah 58:1-66:24
Week 43	Jun 19 - Jun 25	Psalms 114:1-119:8
Week 44	Jun 26 - Jul 2	Psalms 119:9-119:64
Week 45	Jul 3 - Jul 9	Psalms 119:65-119:120
Week 46	Jul 10 - Jul 16	Psalms 119:121-119:176
Week 47	Jul 17 - Jul 23	Romans 1:1-3:20
Week 48	Jul 24 - Jul 30	Romans 3:21-6:23
Week 49	Jul 31 - Aug 6	Romans 7:1-9:33
Week 50	Aug 7 - Aug 13	Romans 10:1-12:21
Week 51	Aug 14 - Aug 20	Romans 13:1-16:27
Week 52	Aug 21 - Aug 27	Hosea 3:4-14:19